The Art of Learning to LOVe YOURSELF

The Art of Learning to Love Yourself

CECIL G. OSBORNE

**ZONDERVAN
PUBLISHING HOUSE** OF THE ZONDERVAN CORPORATION
GRAND RAPIDS, MICHIGAN 49506

THE ART OF LEARNING TO LOVE YOURSELF

Copyright © 1976 by The Zondervan Corporation
Grand Rapids, Michigan

Second printing 1977

Library of Congress Cataloging in Publication Data
Osborne Cecil G
  The art of learning to love yourself.

  1. Self-respect.   I. Title.
BF697.073   158'.1   76-23231

Grateful acknowledgment is made to the following for occasional Scripture quotations. The source is indicated in each instance.

AMERICAN BIBLE SOCIETY, *The New Testament in Today's English.* Copyright © 1966 by The American Bible Society.

DIVISION OF CHRISTIAN EDUCATION, NATIONAL COUNCIL OF CHURCHES OF CHRIST IN THE UNITED STATES OF AMERICA. *The Revised Standard Version of the Bible,* 2nd ed. Copyright © 1972 by the Division of Christian Education, National Council of Churches of Christ in the United States of America.

TYNDALE HOUSE PUBLISHERS. *The Living Bible: Paraphrased* by Kenneth Taylor. Copyright © 1971 by Tyndale House Publishers.

Printed in the United States of America.

Contents

Preface

An ancient monarch called together the wise men and philosophers of his kingdom and instructed them to compile all the wisdom of the ages. They labored for twenty years on this prodigious task. Finally they came before the king, bearing forty large leather-bound volumes. He examined them. "Condense it," he said. "It's too long."

The scholars worked for two years and returned with one huge volume. The king said: "It's much too large and forbidding a book. Condense it." The dispirited scholars returned to their libraries, labored for three months and returned to the palace bearing a very small piece of paper containing a single sentence. "This is the condensed wisdom of the ages, distilled into a single sentence," their spokesman said.

The king read it, and his face lit up. "Wonderful!" he said. "This is it." The paper read: "There are no free lunches."

The profundity of that lies in the implication that nothing is free; there is no such thing as magic, and there are few simple solutions. Everything has its price in terms of effort, discipline, money, or time.

An American visitor at an ancient English castle asked the head gardener how he managed to produce such a magnificent lawn. The old gentleman removed his pipe, looked down thoughtfully at the deep velvety grass and said, "Well, we just planted it, fertilized it regularly, watered and tended it carefully for four hundred years." Any worthwhile project takes time.

While it is relatively simple to name the steps by which one can achieve a greater degree of self-love (self-approval, a better self-image, self-acceptance, self-esteem), it is somewhat more

7

difficult to apply these principles. Reading the formula will not suffice. One must work at it diligently and faithfully, and the task must be given priority.

In order to learn to like or love yourself, you must first find out who you are, and how you became the person you are. Your name is not your identity. Nor is your role as mother, father, student, employee. You are much more than your role in life.

Many people believe that they know themselves well. Yet they seldom do. As Dr. Paul Tournier points out, we can never know ourselves fully; but we can begin the process of discovering somewhat more completely who we are.

Paradoxically, we come to know ourselves *in the act of self-disclosure*. A little girl, asked what she thought about something, said, "How do I know what I think until I hear what I have to say?" In disclosing ourselves to "significant others" we discover our true identity.

Talking *about* oneself in a narcissistic manner is not self-disclosure. The true sharing of one's inner self can take place only in a setting where openness and honesty are encouraged, where there is no possibility of being judged or criticized. The dialogue takes place best with a person or persons who will listen to, and affirm, the one sharing. Some sharing groups provide this opportunity.

A book, at best, can provide one with insights, stimulate one's thinking, and suggest a course of action. It is very rarely that the mere reading of a book and giving intellectual assent to some concepts has changed lives. But I have read books that stimulated me, opened new vistas, and offered a new course of action. The rest was up to me.

Most of us are somewhat lazy, or tend to procrastinate. (It was reported that the National Society of Procrastinators had planned to meet in San Francisco last month, but decided to postpone their meeting for a year.) Discipline — doing what we ought, when we should, whether we feel like it or not — is seldom easy.

The art of learning to love ourselves involves, first, discovering how, as children, we learned to dislike ourselves; then through diligent effort we can learn to love ourselves properly. When we shall have achieved that, our relationships will begin to improve. Liking ourselves better, we discover a new and wonderful self-acceptance, and become capable of giving and receiving love.

1 Most People Dislike Themselves Whether They Know It or Not

1 Most People Dislike Themselves Whether They Know It or Not

Life is like an onion. You take off one layer at a
time, and sometimes you cry.

— *Carl Sandburg*

She was a normal, thirty-eight-year-old woman, lying on a foam-rubber mat in a soundproof room, but she sounded exactly like a very small child.

"Mommy! Daddy! Where are you? Why don't you come?" she screamed, her face contorting like that of a little girl in anguish.

"I need you! Please, please won't somebody come! I'm scared. Mommy, mommy, mommy!" More heartrending cries and half-stifled sobs. "They've gone away. They don't want me; you don't like me. Mommy, mommy, please come!" That continued for forty-five minutes. Finally she opened her eyes, took a deep breath, and said in her adult voice, "My, that was scary! I was a tiny baby all alone in the crib. The room was dark. I was frightened half out of my mind. I was abandoned, or at least felt like it. Perhaps they had just gone to the other end of the house, but I needed them. I felt lost and scared, and no one came. There is no more awful feeling than that. All I wanted was for someone to pick me up and cuddle me. How desperately I needed that! I felt I would die if someone didn't come."

She was describing a primal experience. I had regressed her

11

to childhood, and she relived this experience of feeling abandoned as an infant. Perhaps most children experience that or something akin to it.

"The feeling," she said, "is that they have gone away forever. They'll never come back. I'm bad. They hate me, or they would come and pick me up."

One part of her mind, as on a split screen, was reliving a childhood experience. The adult portion of her mind knew where she was, and was "listening in," as the infant screamed her feelings of terror and loneliness. She could have returned to the present at any time had she desired to do so, but something kept her in the primal experience. "I wanted to see what happened," she said. "I wondered if they would ever come. They never did, and I gave up. The feeling was, 'They don't love me. I'm worthless.'"

THE ORIGIN OF SELF-HATE

From listening to many hundreds of primal experiences, we have learned that, though parents may love the child, if there is too little holding and cuddling and too much criticism and scolding, the child invariably feels, "They don't like me. I am bad. I will do *anything* if they will only love me; but nothing works. They hate me. I am worthless. I hate myself."

We dislike ourselves because in infancy and childhood we experienced such feelings as these:

They don't want me.
I'm no good.
I'm not supposed to cry. It makes them angry when I cry.
I'll be punished if I'm not quiet (good).
They hate me. I hate myself.
It bothers them when I make a noise.
They must never know what I'm feeling; it upsets them.
If they hit me, I mustn't cry.
They hate me unless I'm good (quiet).
I hate myself because I can't always be good.
I'm worthless; scared; lonely; guilty.

These and scores of other feelings have been verbalized with intensity in thousands of hours of primal experiences[1] at the Burlingame Counseling Center, associated with Yokefellows, Inc.[2] The pain relived and expressed in tears, sobs, and screams reveal the reason adults so often hate themselves: they felt hated as infants and small children because they were not loved in a manner they could accept. They felt unloved because they were not held, cuddled, touched; or because they were screamed at, beaten, scolded, and told in a hundred different ways that they were bad, a nuisance, stupid, wrong.

HOLDING DOWN PRIMAL PAIN

It is widely recognized that the child's personality is formed by the age of four or five, certainly by six. I did not know what enormous scars childhood Pain[3] could leave until, in conducting In-Depth sessions with patients, I heard them relive their hurts hour by hour, hurt by hurt, scream by scream. The reliving of such traumas discharges the tension and anxiety encapsulating the childhood Pain.

It is as though you were standing in a swimming pool, holding down a number of inflated beach balls and feeling that if one ever reaches the surface, it will be disastrous. At the same time, you are trying to carry on a conversation with people around the edge of the pool. The psychic energy used in that game of repression is unbelievable. Small wonder that we are so tired and preoccupied, so tense and anxious and fearful of something unknown.

It is largely because of early primal hurts that people dislike themselves. The harsh parental criticism, spoken or implied, becomes the child's conviction: "I am stupid." The parental expression of irritation or disgust becomes the child's feeling: "I'm no good. I irritate people."

I dealt with this primal Pain and experienced it in all its force many years ago in a therapy group. One member of the group was a supersweet, placid, repressed young woman who had numerous phobias. Using a technique that has since been refined through thousands of hours of experience, I had the compliant young woman beat a large sofa cushion that I held in front of me. She got it on the floor and continued beating it, screaming all the while to her mother, "I hate you, I hate you!" Then she screamed at her father until she was exhausted. She had never expressed the slightest antagonism toward either parent until then. All hostility had been repressed.

She said later, "That felt great! I never knew all that hate was in me! I didn't know I hated anyone. I was never allowed to use the word *hate* or express anger. I had to say only nice things to people, and only pleasant things about them. I never talked back to my parents." She had a large number of additional sessions in private before a lifetime of repressed anger was discharged.

Her phobias and obsessive-compulsive behavior began to diminish as she was relieved of the burden of repressing her primal Pain. Repression leads to obsession. In her case she had repressed so much hurt and anger that her obsessive behavior became almost unendurable.

What is it that parents do to children that causes them to repress their true feelings? And how can children be allowed to express all of their "unacceptable feelings"? Let's take up the last question first.

HANDLING "UNACCEPTABLE" FEELINGS

We have three choices: *To express feelings*, which may or not be appropriate at a particular time; *to suppress* those feelings, meaning to be aware of them, but also to realize it is not appropriate to express them just then; or to *repress* them, bury them, deny that they exist, and then struggle to keep those "guilty," unacceptable feelings in the unconscious, at the cost of real damage to the personality. Childhood hurts that we were not allowed to express are simply added to the pool of primal Pain. It becomes "stored pain," which will ultimately express itself in emotional or physical symptoms.

The mother of a small child was embarrassed when her youngster began screaming in a store. He wanted a toy he saw on the counter. The mother didn't know just what to do, and, not wanting to spank him, allowed him to roll on the floor screaming. A crowd gathered, and angry muttering was heard about what a rotten mother she was.

Embarrassed by the commotion and the criticism, she dragged the screaming child to the car and closed the windows. When he subsided, she said, "Jimmy, I can understand your wanting that toy. It's okay to want it; but it's not all right to scream like that in public. People don't understand. Any time you want to cry, let me know and we will go off by ourselves and you can cry all you need to."

A few days later, having experienced a disappointment at home, he told his mother that he felt like crying. She said, "All right, let's go into the bedroom and you can cry and be just as mad as you feel like." He had a good cry, and when he finished, she hugged him. He was learning that crying was an all-right thing, in the right place. That is a vast improvement over the standard phrase, "Stop crying (stop hurting) or I'll give you something to cry about!"

PARENTAL "PUT-DOWNS" DO PERMANENT DAMAGE

From hundreds of counselees I had heard parent "put-downs," and I asked some of them to list the ones that they resented the most. I have selected some pertinent ones, and by way of a response have indicated what the child *might* have said if he/she had possessed sufficient adult vocabulary and the courage to risk being severely punished or sent to his/her room in disgrace. These verbal put-downs, with fantasized responses, help explain how we got the way we are.

Parent: Don't interrupt me! I'm talking.

Child: So you are. I'm sorry; but how about the ten thousand times you've interrupted me? Why is it okay for you to interrupt me any time, any place, but not all right for me to interrupt you? It ought to work both ways, shouldn't it? Maybe if you'd ever say you're sorry when you interrupt me, I could learn some good manners from your example.

Parent: Do it now. Right now, I tell you!

Child: All right, all right! But why do you expect instant obedience from me, but you never shout, "Do it now!" to each other? And when I ask you for something, you nearly always say, "Wait a minute, I'm busy," or "I'll do it when I get good and ready." And yesterday you screamed at me, "Get off my back, for heaven's sake!" But *I* always have to do it *now*, this very minute. No matter what I'm doing, I have to stop and do what *you* want me to do. I don't understand big people. I don't think I like them. Sometimes I think they're crazy.

Parent: Wait till your father gets home!

Child: Yeah, I've heard that one before! It's about five hours until he gets home, and meanwhile I have to live under a big black cloud of fear. Do you know how long five hours is to a little kid? It's like about five days for you. How would you like to live for the next five days with a threat hanging over your head, and all you know is that something awful is going to happen. You wouldn't like that, would you? You know what? I think you're sadistic, that's what. Either that or just plain mean. If you think I need to be punished, why don't you do it yourself and get it over with? And then I wouldn't have to wait five whole days to find out if dad's going to beat up on me. I don't think I like you. Not at all. But I'm going to

pretend I do, because if I don't, I lose my security. And I
need that something awful.

Parent: Run and get me the hammer.

Child: Look! Why do I always have to *run* and get things for you?
Run down to the store. Run and tell your father. Run and ask
your sister. Run and get me the screwdriver. Run, run, run.
I'm sick of running. *You* people don't run. You walk! Slow-
like. You take it easy. But I'm supposed to be just a speeding
blur as I rush around carrying messages, getting tools, running errands. I'll go on running my legs off just to make sure
I'm loved while I need great gobs of it; but wait till I get
bigger. Then I'm not going to run for anybody. I'll take my
own sweet time. I may even overreact, and act slow and
stupid just to win *one* power struggle. Or, it could fix me so I
go on rushing around all the rest of my life, tense and
anxious, with a big fat anxiety neurosis eating at my gut,
gulping tranquilizers to keep the anxiety down. How'd you
like to be ordered around by *me?* Huh? Run and get my
breakfast, mom. Dad, run and get me that toy you promised
me. Look you two; it ought to work both ways. Only it
doesn't. Wait till I'm real big, say twelve or sixteen, and you
know what? I'll find ways to get even. I could rebel against
all authority, and really get back at you. I'll find ways.

Parent: God doesn't love you when you're bad.

Child: Bad? Am I bad? Does God love me when I'm good and get
mad at me — like you do — when I make a mistake? If he's
like that, he's no better than you are! And if God hates me
when I blow it, then he's mad at you too, because last
Sunday the minister read that part in the Bible where it says,
"All have sinned," and that means you. And if sinning gets
God mad at you, you're in big trouble. When you two get
mad, and yell at each other, does God get mad at you? If so,
he's mad at you a lot of the time. By the way, how come it's
all right for you to get mad but not okay for me to get angry?
Tell me that, huh?

Parent: Tell Jimmy you're sorry. Tell him!

Child: O.K., O.K., but I'm *not* sorry. Not in the slightest. He hit
me first and I'm not sorry I hit him; but if I don't lie and tell
him I'm sorry, you'll hit *me*. So I'll lie about it, and that way I
won't get hit. Why is it I have to tell Jimmy I'm sorry when I
hit him in self-defense, and you never say you're sorry when
you hit me? How come, huh?

Parent: Look at those grades!

Child: Yeah, just look at them. Keep on looking till you see if you can figure out why they're so rotten. I'll tell you. Kids all want to learn. It's built into us; but with you two quarreling and threatening to split up, you've got my nerves all shot. I can't concentrate; I can't even remember assignments the teacher gives. I go to school with a knot in my stomach half the time, and then my brains don't work. When you aren't arguing about who's right and who's wrong, you fight about money and ten thousand other things I don't understand. All I know is that I've got this big knot in my stomach, and I feel anxious all the time. And another thing: The time I brought home three A's and two B's, and a C, you said, "All right, but you can do better." Did I get any recognition for knocking myself out to get those grades? No! You just kept setting the goals higher. I didn't like that, you know it? And so next time I got C's, a couple of D's, and two F's.

Parent: This hurts me more than it does you.

Child: You've got to be kidding! Or stupid. Kids don't buy that garbage. I know what you feel when you're beating up on me. You're feeling angry and frustrated because you have such a poor idea of what it means to raise kids, and you project your self-hatred onto me, and beat up on me just because you're an incompetent parent. I know I make mistakes, but is that any excuse to go knocking me around? You call it a spanking. To me it's a beating, because that's what it feels like. Look, when you make a mistake does someone beat up on you? Any dumb parent can start beating a kid, but it takes a concerned parent to go to the library and check out a few books on child rearing. If you spent as much time studying how to be a good parent as you do watching TV, you might learn how some punishment just makes me resentful and rebellious, and how I unconsciously decide to punish *you* in some way, by doing something really bad.

Parent: Stop crying, or I'll give you something to cry about.

Child: All right, if you say so. I have no other choice. So what I'll do is this: I'll bury my hurt and grief and anger, bury it so deep no one will ever know what I'm feeling. I'll bury my joy and spontaneity, too. I'll wall myself in so I won't feel much of anything. I'll become an unfeeling person, that's what I'll do. I'll substitute cynicism for the buried feelings I'm not allowed to express. I may get migraine headaches, or depression, or some other symptoms, but at least I won't have to *feel.*

Parent: You must respect your parents.

Child: Yeah, why? You don't respect me. You scream at me, hit me, and tell me how bad I am, or how silly or stupid or clumsy. If you did that to your friends, you'd lose all of them. You *have* to be polite to *them,* even when you don't really like what they're doing. You respect them enough not to insult them. And you know what? Some of them are real weirdos. I've heard you say so in private, but you're nice to them to their faces. If I acted that weird, you'd *really* let me have it! No, you don't respect me, and frankly I don't respect you, either. But I have to play along with you, because you're bigger than I am, and I need you for the time being. Until I get bigger. Then watch out!

Parent: Don't touch yourself down there!

Child: Oh? Is there something wrong with that part of my body? Is it bad or evil down there? I thought God made all of me. If he did, how come part of me is bad or dirty? Okay, I'll repress my sexuality and come to think of sex as dirty, something you don't talk about, but just tell dirty stories about. And by the way, if sex is dirty, what about some of the magazines I see around the house? Is sex something only big people can talk about? What's the big secret? If there's something you're trying to keep from me, I am going to find out what it is, one way or another. Soon.

Parent: Don't you dare talk back to me!

Child: Why not? You two talk back to each other. Loud, too. You shout and argue or go into big angry silences that are worse than the shouting. Sometimes you use some words you told me were bad, and said I shouldn't use. How come you argue and scream at each other, and if I say one little word back I get hit?

Parent: I don't know what will ever become of you!

Child: If you don't, who does? I'm just a little kid, so how would I know? But if you keep on predicting failure for me, I'll really get to believe I'm a no-good, rotten kid like you say. Your questions become my doubts. And my doubts will become fear, and fear will become a certainty, and I *will* fail just like you programmed me.

Parent: Did you do that? If you did, I'm going to punish you!

Child: Don't be silly. I'm not going to confess. I'm going to lie about it, like any normal, red-blooded American kid who doesn't want to get beaten up. Because sometimes when I lie, I get away with it; but if I confess, I get knocked all over the place. And when you tell me I won't get punished if I tell the truth, and I confess, then I get a gosh-awful lecture lasting a good hour; and you keep referring to it for days after. I'd rather take my chance on the lie and maybe not getting a whipping. And I'll probably go on lying because when I'm accused, my automatic response is to defend myself. You lie too. I've heard you lie to people lots of times. And I heard you two scheming about the income tax. Was that a lie, or wasn't it? And did anyone beat you up for it? So why do I get hit when I tell a lie? Accuse me enough and I'll become a professional, gold-plated, pathological liar, like you say Uncle Ted is.

Parent: Sit still! Stop squirming! You must be quiet in church, do you hear?

Child: At my age, you expect me, just a little kid, to sit still while someone gives with all that heavy theological stuff? That's a real head trip, if you ask me. I'm bored out of my skull. I'll bet you were, too, when you went to church as a little kid, no matter how God-fearing and rigid you may be now. Look, suppose you went to a lecture by a nuclear physicist and he talked about how $E = MC^2$ operates in relation to the ions in a given molecule and what that does to a bunch of isotopes. Would you sit still and listen to that for three hours? That's how long your hour seems to me. Church isn't geared to kids, for Pete's sake! My legs don't even reach the floor. How would you like to sit on a hard seat for hours with your legs dangling?

Another thing. Take that sandbox I used to play in when I was in the nursery at Sunday school. How come playing in the sandbox at church is religious, and playing in a sandbox at kindergarten is secular? How about that?

And something else. I noticed how godly you two look sitting in church, but you didn't sound so pious the other day when you were yelling at each other. And how about that time you two didn't speak to each other for four whole days? And I've heard some pretty rough language coming out of both of you, words you tell me not to use. No matter what you tell me to do or not do, I'm going to grow up imitating you. You ought to know that.

I love you, but I think you're phonies. That asthma I had, remember? And the colic earlier, and the breaking out? You know what caused that? I'll tell you. It was because of all the tension I picked up in this family. And those bad dreams I used to have came from the conflict I feel in this house. I really do love you, mainly because I need you, but I hate your talking one way and acting another. It bothers me.

The child's self-image is being formed in his early years. He either learns that he is loved, that he is a great kid, basically good, doing his best, and is going to succeed in life, or that he is not loved, but impatiently endured, that he is bad or stupid, and will probably come to a bad end.

The Double Bind

It is equally frustrating and damaging to put the child in a double bind. George, a delightful but unbelievably tense and anxious man of forty said, "My mother kept asking me as a child why I didn't talk. I didn't know why, of course. She used to say, 'You never talk! What's the matter with you?' I could only imagine that there was something wrong with me, but when I tried to say something, she would invariably jump down my throat, always showing me where I was wrong, or why I shouldn't feel the way I did. There was no way I could win with her."

The Fetus Is a *Person*, Who Feels!

Life begins, not just at birth, but before birth. An unborn child can learn, feel pain, acquire likes and dislikes, and even become bored in the womb, according to Professor William Liley of Auckland University. He stated in a lecture, "The process of learning to suck, to drink, to use one's lungs and limbs, begins in the womb, in one environment, in preparation for emergence into another environment at birth." He went on to say that "the unborn child is responsive to pain and touch, to cold and sound and light. He gets hiccups and sucks his thumb. He winks and sleeps. He gets bored with repetitive signals but can be taught to be alerted by a first signal or a different one." Sir William's conclusions were based on experiments with unborn children at

Auckland University, New Zealand.

There is considerable evidence, too, that the unborn child feels very much what the mother feels. Her anxiety, or fear, happiness or depression, are felt by the child, since, after all, the child is still part of the mother.

Dr. Frederick Leboyer, author of *Birth Without Violence*,[4] stated in an interview that in his opinion the child is "conscious from the moment of conception."

Whether or not one is prepared to accept that without question, it is generally conceded that the first few years of life are of enormous importance. We cannot be certain of all the forces that were brought to bear upon us in those earliest years, since far more than nine-tenths of all that transpired from birth to age five has been buried; but what transpired in those early years formed us and made us what we are.

It is not only the verbal put-downs that damage a child. An unfeeling parent, unable to express love, can produce a child whose feelings are blocked; and the results range from anxiety, depression, and general ineffectiveness to mental illness.

WE ARE ALL DAMAGED

Without knowing all of the details, we can sense the general outline: all of us, even in the most enlightened and loving home environment, were damaged to some extent; for as there are no perfect parents, there is no perfect environment and thus there are no perfect children grown into adults.

We dislike ourselves in direct proportion to the amount of rejection and criticism we experienced in childhood. We like and accept ourselves to the degree that our parents loved and accepted us — *in a manner we could accept.*

Bland, unfeeling, nontouching parents produce children who tend to feel unworthy and self-rejecting. They find it hard to accept compliments, and experience an excessive amount of free-floating anxiety. The infant who was not held or cuddled or affirmed will become an adult with deep anxiety, and physical or emotional problems. As Erich Fromm has pointed out, we learn to love by having been loved.[5] Very often an individual is limited in self-love because as a child there was little or no love shown. In the early part of this century the school of "behaviorism" flourished for a time and had a great deal of damaging influence upon the children of those who followed behaviorist principles.

In order to understand the behaviorist school of thought

fully, consider the following statement by Dr. J. B. Watson, its founder:

> Mothers just don't know, when they kiss their children and pick them up and rock them, caress them and jiggle them upon their knee, that they are slowly building up a human being totally unable to cope with the world it must later live in. . . . There is a sensible way of treating children. Treat them as though they were young adults. . . . Never hug or kiss them, never let them sit on your lap. If you must, kiss them on the forehead when they say goodnight. . . . Can't a mother train herself to substitute a kindly word, a smile, in all her dealings with the child, for the kiss and the hug, the pickup and the coddlings? . . . If you haven't a nurse and cannot leave the child, put it out in the back yard a large part of the day. Build a fence around the yard so that you are sure no harm can come to it. Do this from the time it is born. . . . If your heart is too tender and you must watch the child, make yourself a peephole so that you can see it without being seen, or use a periscope. . . . Finally, learn not to talk in endearing and coddling terms.[6]

Many parents who are horrified by such an approach to child rearing have done irreparable harm to their children by alternating between overpermissiveness and punitiveness, by excessive criticism, and in a thousand other ways. Most of us, in fact, have been damaged to some extent, large or small, by well-meaning parents who firmly believed they loved us, yet who failed to display it in the simplest and most fundamental ways — by touching and cuddling, by praise and affirmation.

Such people cannot like or love themselves, because they were not loved in a way they could readily accept. Parents often send a double message: the verbal message is "You know how much we love you, dear; just see all the things we do for you, and all we've given you, not to mention the sacrifices we've made for you," but the message the child receives may develop these feelings:

> You don't love me, because you never hold me or cuddle me.
> You yell at me all the time, then tell me you love me.
> I get a hundred criticisms for every word of approval, so I must be no good. I am not loved.

Mother's actions may belie her words; her tone of voice may be in total disagreement with what she says. The child of such a parent may grow up to be a nontoucher, afraid of giving or receiving love, suspicious of people's motives, cold and aloof; or, depending upon numerous factors, he may become effusive and gushy, overcompliant, sending out messages of insincerity, while feeling inwardly, "Love me, accept me, tell me I'm all right; touch me, affirm me, make up for all the loving and touching I failed to receive as a child."

Cultures and religions of all varieties have sought a common goal: the Nirvana of the Buddhists, the Satori of Zen, the Samadhi of the Hindus, the "peace that passes understanding" of the Christians. Could this longing for infinite peace and serenity be, not simply the reaction to life's stress, but an echo of the peace once experienced before birth? Or is it rather the haunting preconception memory of at-oneness experienced in a prebirth experience, when we were one with the Father? No one can say with finality. All that is certain is that we are here, that we were damaged in some degree, that we are all different, and that we must learn to live together, to communicate more effectively, to love more deeply, or we shall all perish together.

Notes

[1]An explanation of In-Depth Therapy dealing with primal feelings will be found in Appendix A.

[2]19 Park Road, Burlingame, CA 94010.

[3]"Pain" here is capitalized to indicate that we are dealing with something of almost unbelievable enormity: the devastating shock of feeling such emotions as rejection, ridicule, disappointment, threats, and deprivation of love.

[4]Frederick Le boyer, *Birth Without Violence* (New York: Alfred A. Knopf, 1975).

[5]Eric Fromm, *The Art of Loving* (New York: Harper and Row, 1956).

[6]J. B. Watson, *Psychological Care of Infant and Child* (New York: Norton & Co., 1928).

2 How We Got That Way

2 How We Got That Way

You have no idea what a poor opinion I have of
myself — and how little I deserve it.

— *W. S. Gilbert*

Stanley, a delightful minister in his forties, related this incident at
a Yokefellow retreat:

It was his first day at school, and he was quite proud of the
fact that he could write his name. The teacher invited him to
demonstrate. He spelled it out in block letters: STANLEY. She
said, "You spelled it wrong. It's spelled Standley." He replied,
"No ma'am, there is no *d* in my name." She said sternly, "Write
it again, and spell it right this time!"

Stanley wrote it correctly again, without the *d*. She
scooped up the paper, held it before the class and said, "Look,
class; here's a boy who's so stupid he doesn't even know how to
spell his own name. Now, Stanley, write your name again and put
a *d* in it, do you hear?" And he did, raging inside as he wrote it.

"That scene is stamped on my mind forever," he said. "I
cringe and hurt inside every time I think of it, because the class
laughed when she told them how stupid I was; and for some
reason I accepted her evaluation.

"So, to this day I feel stupid. I know in my head I am not, but
I *feel* stupid. Not long ago I was counseling with a man who had a
Ph.D. He seemed pleased with the results of our session and said,

'You know, I always felt you had a lot on the ball; now I'm convinced.' My immediate reaction was, 'You must be pretty dumb yourself not to see how stupid and inadequate I really am.' "

Thus are our personalities formed or malformed.

SIBLING RIVALRY

Marilyn, a married woman in her late thirties, had come with her husband to discuss their marital relationship. I sensed more anxiety in her than could be accounted for by her current situation. When she had her first individual session, I encouraged her to try a primal experience to see what we could uncover.

She was so emotionally blocked that it was difficult to get her into anything very deep at first, but at one point she became very agitated. Finally she opened her eyes and said in astonishment, "Why, she tried to kill me! My own sister!"

What she had experienced was a childhood event, part of which her parents had related to her. As the mother had described it, Marilyn had been riding her tricycle on the front porch in the care of her older sister. Her mother heard the screech of brakes, rushed to the door and saw the child on her tricycle out in the middle of a busy thoroughfare with cars backed up in both directions. She rushed out and rescued her. Marilyn had no conscious memory of the experience.

In her first primal session she had gone back and relived that event in its entirety. It was not remembered, but *relived*, with all the intensity of the original occurrence.

"I saw her push me down the steps and felt the bumping of the tricycle as it went down the steps and off the curb and out into the street. I relived the entire event. She tried to kill me! I knew she had always hated me, and still does, but I had no idea she had done *that*." Reliving the experience and discovering what had actually transpired helped her understand many things about her childhood.

How can one be sure these are not childhood fantasies? The answer is that one who relives such events *knows;* and, significantly, many repressed memories that have been relived by individuals in primals have been verified by parents or others in a position to know the facts.

Not all children react to the birth of a younger brother or sister in the same way. Some older siblings seem genuinely to rejoice, while others display an unbelievable hostility. This can be understood if we look at it this way: Little Mary is an only child. She has been the princess, the sole object of parental affection. Then one day the announcement is made: "You're going to have a little baby sister, or brother. Isn't that wonderful?"

The parents are excited and happy. The little princess takes the cue from the parents' feelings, and decides to try to be happy too. Then little brother/sister is brought home. Now attention is divided (and not very evenly divided). That little interloper, that pretender to the crown becomes the focal point of parental attention. The princess is dethroned.

A parallel would be for a husband to announce to his wife, "Darling, I am going to bring home a wonderful playmate for you. She's somewhat younger than you, and *very beautiful*. You two are going to live together in our home, and *you're going to love her*. I'm going to love you both equally, though at first I'll be paying a great deal of attention to her." What the wife would feel about such an event is precisely what many children feel when a new baby is brought home.

One woman assured me that the birth of her little brother had posed no problem for her. "I genuinely loved little Bobby," she said.

In a primal session she relived an experience when she was three — the birth of her brother Bobby. She went into a rage lasting over an hour. Then she wept. What little love she had been receiving now went to Bobby.

For the first time she saw why she always went into an unreasoning and uncontrollable rage when her husband showed affection to his daughter by a previous marriage. The daughter represented Bobby, who had taken away the love she desperately needed at age three.

"I never felt anything like that when my baby sister/brother was brought home" is a common response. I neither believe nor disbelieve that. Children learn very early that in order to survive they must deny feelings that might evoke parental displeasure. The child is totally dependent upon parental favor and does not know, yet, that he/she had a perfect right to any and all feelings.

It is not only parental "put-downs," sibling rivalry, or abuse and ridicule from authority figures that leave their mark. There are a thousand subtle forces impinging upon the delicate and sensitive fabric of the small child's emotional structure.

"Don't Touch Yourself Down There"

A young man whom I had known most of his life came to

discuss with me a major crisis facing him. His wife wanted a divorce, and he was devastated. They had been married only a few years, and he was very much in love with her.

One major complaint his wife had voiced was that he was virtually sexually impotent. There were other factors, but this one loomed large. He wanted to know whether his impotence was physical or entirely psychological. I told him that in one his age the problem was nearly always psychological.

He did feel vaguely reticent about sex, he told me, as though there was "something wrong, or bad, or dirty" about it. I told him that in many instances the mother is disturbed when a child touches the genital area. A typical reaction is for the mother to snatch the hand away, or slap it, and say, "Stop that! That's dirty! Don't touch yourself down there."

He gasped in surprise. "I've seen my mother do that many times with my little sister, and she must have done it with me!"

"Then," I said, "the child is conditioned to feel that there is something wrong with the genitals. It isn't a thought, or a conviction, just a vague persistent feeling. Some people are able to overcome it, while others are seriously affected by it."

I asked him how he had felt about masturbation as a boy. "Terrible," he said. "That was something awful. I don't know precisely how or when or where I got the message, but I sensed that masturbation was forbidden, wrong, a sin against God."

"Do you still feel that way?"

"Yes, I think I do. There's something vaguely bad about it. It *is* wrong, isn't it?"

I explained that most enlightened medical men, ministers, psychiatrists, and psychologists agree that there is absolutely nothing wrong with masturbation. It is, as Charlie Shedd expresses it in his excellent book *The Stork Is Dead,* "God's gift to the young"[1] and, one might add, to the unmarried. He looked surprised at this totally new piece of information.

For many centuries children were savagely punished when suspected of what was termed "the solitary vice of self-abuse." The origin of this taboo is lost in antiquity, but it is known to be thousands of years old. *The Egyptian Book of the Dead* (1550 to 950 B.C.) refers to masturbation in negative terms.

Religious and medical authorities cooperated in trying to stamp out masturbation. Some medical men, until the early part of this century, thought it was the cause of mental illness.

No one knows how many women have found themselves

sexually frigid, or partly so, as the result of misinformation of this sort, together with anxious cautioning calculated to prevent an unwanted pregnancy. After repeated warnings not to "touch yourself down there" (much of it before the age of conscious memory), coupled with anxiety transmitted by parents about "getting into trouble," many women feel great anxiety and confusion about sex. A few minutes at the altar cannot erase mental and emotional conditioning that may begin in infancy and continue for years.

And much of the conditioning is not verbal. Where sex is seldom if ever mentioned in the home, children frequently grow up with a vague feeling that some monumental secret is being kept from them. If they seek to fathom the mystery on their own, they are often punished or made to feel guilty.

We can like ourselves better and relate better to people when we understand ourselves and the factors that made us the way we are. When we see the manifold ways in which personalities can be warped and damaged, it makes it easier to view ourselves and others with amused, friendly tolerance.

There Is No One to Blame

A kind word needs to be said about parents at this point. There is little organized effort to teach parents how to raise children. It is possible to get credit for a course in archery in numerous colleges and universities. One New York state college has offered a course in handicapping; that is, how to study racing forms and come to some conclusion as to which horse is most likely to win a given race. One may learn about rice tonnage in Indochina, the ocean currents adjacent to the Cape of Good Hope, fourth-century-B.C. Chinese art, the names of assorted kings and a hundred wars. But relatively few courses are offered in either high school or college to prepare one for marriage and child rearing, two of the most complex tasks ever to face a human being.

Falling in love has little or nothing to do with working out a good marriage relationship, and conceiving a child bears little or no relationship to the arduous eighteen-year task of rearing a child. Yet in our present culture it is assumed that falling in love is the main thing — which it isn't — and that child rearing will take care of itself — which it seldom does.

Neurotic Perfectionism

It is not only verbal abuse, or neglect, that traumatizes

children. They can be damaged by overmothering, by perfectionism, and unrealistic praise.

Jean was dying of cancer in her mid-thirties when I first met her. It took a long time for her to die, and during those tragic years she had ample time to think. She told me one day, "Of course, I can't prove that there is any connection between my illness and my mother's attitude, but I feel deep down that there's some definite relationship. My mother always insisted that her children were perfect. I can still hear her giving smiling, confident assurance to friends and relatives that 'all my children are perfect.' We all tried to live up to that. We knew that we weren't perfect, of course, and I think this created a terrible conflict between the knowledge that we were imperfect kids like everyone else and the goal of perfection that mother set for us.

"It has been an intolerable burden all my life. I feel that this conflict I have lived with so long is somehow related to my cancer."

Her mother had either been attempting to stress the positive to an absurd degree, or else she simply blinded herself to the possibility that *her* children could be other than perfect, in which case she could not get credit for being a perfect mother.

Gwen had a different feeling about her childhood and her parents. She is a lovely young woman in her early thirties, intelligent but emotionally rigid. She told me in a counseling session, "I know intellectually that it isn't true, but I *feel* very strongly that my parents are perfect. I know they aren't, but they *seem* perfect." They had not tried to convince her that *she* was perfect; far from it. But they managed to convey to her that they were utterly beyond question and perfect as parents.

There was no point in trying to disillusion her, for feelings are not directly available to logic. When her parents became hopeless alcoholics and phoned her repeatedly in the middle of the night to settle some drunken argument, the myth began to be dispelled from her emotional nature. And when her father committed suicide in her mother's presence, the ancient childhood illusion of parental perfection finally exploded; but the damage had been done.

Our goal at this point is to cease blaming ourselves for what we have become and to avoid any tendency to blame our parents. Whatever their faults, they were at least partially successful. They may have done their best. It does no good to blame them or ourselves for what has transpired. We are responsible only for what we do with our lives from this point on.

The gospel does not condemn us for the weakness and failures resulting from a faulty environment. We are not held responsible for that. We are held responsible only for what we do with our marred, faulty lives from here on out, considering the damaged persons we all are. Christ's cry from the cross "Father, forgive them; for they know not what they do" (Luke 23:34, RSV) carries with it the implication that their personalities and reactions were formed by a thousand factors. Only God could assess the blame or fix responsibility.

After many thousands of hours of counseling, I find that I never feel critical of an individual after I acquire *all of the available facts about the person's early life*. All I can feel is compassion. This is what the Cross is saying to us!

The Three A's

We cannot like ourselves, nor love ourselves properly, nor relate creatively to others, unless we understand what it is that motivates human beings. Basically the driving force is the need for:

Acceptance
Approval
Affection/Love

To be *accepted* means to be welcomed into the family, the tribe, the clan, the social group. The opposite of this is rejection, one of the most painful of all experiences. Not to be accepted is to be an outcast, a reject. The feeling is "I am not worthy, I am no good; there is something wrong with me." It is a very lonely feeling. Many children, for one reason or another, have felt this loneliness. Adults, who as children did not learn to relate easily to their peers, find this a devastating and depressing ongoing ordeal.

To experience *approval* is to win the affirmation of "significant others." To the child this means approval by the family and close friends. Performance in school, indicated by grades, is one way children gain — or fail to gain — approval. The child usually seeks approval in terms of performance rather than for what he is as a person. It is easier to demonstrate worth with a report card or by performance in sports, in social activities, in music, in something we *do*, than to wait for people to recognize our worth as individuals.

Affection/Love refers to the need to have people express warmth and affection for us, not because of what we do, but because they care about us as persons. Deep within every human there is the need to be loved. Some have found early in life that "love hurts" and have shut the door on this tender emotion. Such people often become cynical. Others compensate by turning their energies into some endeavor where they can be admired, or at least noticed, if not loved. As a last resort, some become criminals in an effort to achieve notoriety in lieu of acceptance or love. In this way they are at least "noticed."

From infancy on, the individual will go to almost any lengths to win approval, acceptance, and/or affection. Failing in this, some persons become depressed and apathetic; others act out their hurt aggressively, while still others become ill in an unconscious effort to gain sympathy or to be taken care of.

The individual who talks interminably about his latest illness is, of course, seeking attention, first cousin to approval. One child in a family may win love and approval by being compliant and obedient. A sibling, finding the compliant slot already filled, may become aggressive and disobedient in an unconscious effort to win at least some attention.

"Notice me!" is the universal cry that goes up from everyone, "if not because I am obedient, or nice, or lovable, then because I make good grades, or because I am good in sports, or *something.*"

SUBSTITUTES FOR LOVE

Some standard compensations for the need to be important, loved, and accepted, are these: the achieving of power, wealth, fame (or notoriety), degrees, titles, badges, citations, blue ribbons at the county fair, wall plaques, certificates — anything to certify that we are significant and worthwhile.

In order to achieve such distinctions, men and women have struggled, sacrificed, fought, schemed, lied, betrayed, and have even attempted acts of heroism and bravery. Others have become "saints"; if nothing else, one can be more godly or more humble, more *something* than others. The eternal silent cry goes up, "Notice me; tell me I am significant."

But when a child has been adequately loved — cuddled, touched, reassured — and nurtured by emotionally mature parents, there is no need for him to manipulate or overcompensate. He is not overly compliant nor overly aggressive. He doesn't *have* to prove anything in order to win love. He *feels* loved and secure.

I would not deprecate the human struggle to achieve and to attain some worthwhile goal. No one wishes to throw cold water on honest human endeavor. But the important thing in the struggle is to *recognize the motivation*. We must be honest with ourselves. Self-delusion is terribly devastating and damaging to the personality.

MEETING-MANIA

For too many years I was engrossed in attending denominational meetings and conventions. A month seldom passed that I did not attend several local, state, or national board meetings. The overriding feeling was that I was taking part in something significant and hopefully doing some good; but in the back of my mind was the partly buried knowledge that I enjoyed sitting in on all those board meetings because it made me feel significant.

For twenty years I made two or more trips from the west coast to the midwest or the east coast every year to attend national board meetings or conventions, and after a number of these I returned home with very bad hay fever symptoms, even in winter. Finally I let myself become aware of the fact that though I enjoyed *being asked* to serve on those boards, I actually *hated the process*. It seemed to me that they often struggled interminably over minor matters that I would have disposed of with a memo dictated to a secretary; or they rushed through matters of immense importance without giving it adequate thought. I simply wasn't on their wavelength nor they on mine.

Eventually, in a burst of self-honesty, I resigned from the national board, then later from state and local boards and committees. After all, I had put in many years at that sort of thing and had served my time. My physical symptoms disappeared when I turned in my resignation. My physical-emotional organism had been wiser than my intellect. As soon as I could recognize my true motivation, which was the need to feel significant, I felt free to function only in areas where I felt comfortable. Honesty with oneself, with God, and with one's fellow-man is the first all-important step in spiritual and emotional growth.

"ROLE" IS NOT "IDENTITY"

If a mother whose children have left the nest can be totally honest with herself, she will not meddle in their lives. She has done her job, well or poorly, as the case may be, and she should cut the cord. She is no longer a "mommy," but ideally a friend of her "former children."

But if she lacks true self-acceptance and has confused the role of mother with her identity, then she will need to counsel them, visit them, correct them and their children, in an effort to feel significant. Meddling mothers usually are those who never had any other identity than that of wife and mother. When deprived of those roles, they tend to feel useless and abandoned and often wallow in self-pity.

Our grown son wrote me one day: "I've decided to promote you. You are no longer my dad, but my *friend*." I felt a wave of deep satisfaction as I read that.

The businessman who has been of value to his firm — and therefore feels significant — will do well to plan ten years in advance for his retirement. The time will come when he will no longer be needed by his firm. As a retired man he loses significance unless he has discovered more meaning to life than working for Amalgamated Tool and Die Company, which, after all, is not an identity.

The people I know who truly like themselves as persons, apart from their roles in life as husband, wife, parent, or jobholder, are those who have learned to be honest with themselves and who to some degree understand themselves. They are able to relate well with others because they like themselves and do not project their own buried self-hate onto those around them. Those who have learned to love themselves properly tend to love others.

A woman in her early forties, with a very strained look, came to our counseling center daily for two-hour primal sessions scheduled to last three weeks. She responded so well to the sessions that she left after two weeks. After several months she wrote me:

> I am finding myself much more spontaneous in relating to people. A few months ago I made a pledge to myself that I would make daily contact with someone outside of my family and job either through a visit, phone call, or letter. I have been amazed at the way in which people have responded to me with unbelievable warmth. I have come to realize that I have never really known any rejection as an adult. Whatever rejection took place in my life happened in childhood. It took me so long to understand that it is only through relating to other people that God's love shines through.
>
> My relationship with members of my family seems to be

growing by leaps and bounds. I find that the more I give, the more love I receive. I have never before experienced such inner peace. I have discovered that I have many God-given qualities that people respond to, and *I like myself*.

She was able to achieve this breakthrough into a proper self-love in twenty-five hours of intensive primal sessions. Some people take longer. During this period she relived the incredibly painful years of her early childhood, the memory of which had been totally buried.

The abandonment by her mother in infancy, the neurotic demands of her father, her own loneliness as a child — all this she relived hour by hour, scene by scene. And in so doing she found the roots of her lifelong depression and the self-rejection that she had projected onto other people.

When she could accept her Pain by reliving it fully, she no longer had to spend half or more of her psychic energy holding down the primal hurts that had blocked her for so many years.

There are no free lunches, no magic cures. There is a price tag on every item. An old Spanish proverb says, "And God said, 'Take what you want and pay for it.'" And the Bible expresses it in these words: "You will seek me and find me; when you seek me with all your heart" (Jeremiah 29:13, RSV).

Notes

[1]Charlie W. Shedd, *The Stork Is Dead* (Waco: Word Books, 1968).

3 How Guilt, Shame, and a Feeling of Inferiority Create a Weak Self-Image

3 How Guilt, Shame, and a Feeling of Inferiority Create a Weak Self-Image

> You ask the meaning of life? Why are we here? It's simple. We're here to discover the meaning of life.
>
> — C. Gillette

When Jeanette was regressed back to early childhood, she saw with startling clarity that she had, as she put it, "married my mother." Her mother was sadistic, and so was her ex-husband. "He told me I was no good, and that was his refrain for twenty years. Mother had abused and neglected me; so I married a man who carried on the tradition. How awful! I never saw that until today."

In a primal session Jeanette relived a period of her childhood when her mother had said repetitiously, "You're so fat and ugly no one will ever notice you or like you. Now go sit in the corner. People want to see your little brother. They don't want to see you." So she sat in a corner getting fatter and lonelier and sadder. Most of this had been totally repressed.

"I'm afraid of life," she said. "If I let myself be loved, I'll be abused and hurt. I saw it today as I relived that part of my childhood. I'm afraid of the calculated risk of love. As a child, if I ever expressed a feeling, mother would shout at me, 'You shouldn't *feel* that way! You're wrong! Go pray about it.' Whatever I said was wrong. I came to associate 'being fat' with being good and being wrong. So I still eat and stay fat to

41

avoid letting anyone love me, because love hurts."

Sigmund Freud pointed out that it is almost impossible to distinguish between the feeling of guilt and the feeling of inferiority. I would add that shame, guilt, inferiority, and failure are different manifestations of the feeling of "worthlessness." Guilt, real or false, is probably the most damaging of all emotions. It is terribly devastating to create in a child needless feelings of guilt, shame, and inferiority. Jesus said to his disciples, "If he were thrown into the sea with a huge rock tied to his neck, he would be far better off than facing the punishment in store for those who harm these little children's souls" (Luke 17:2,3, *Living Bible*).

Most Neuroses Are Rooted in the Past

Jud, about forty, gave up his job and drove 2,500 miles to join a Yokefellow group in California. I said, after a counseling session, "Jud, I'll be glad to put you in a group, but if you want to speed things up, I think it's important to get to the root of your tremendous anxiety. The basis of it almost certainly lies below the level of conscious memory."

He had a series of primal sessions during which he relived long-buried traumas of childhood. One of the first experiences he dealt with was that of looking at his mother one day and wondering, "What would happen if I killed her?" He was seized instantly with a sense of overwhelming guilt. In his primal sessions he wept over and over: "Who can I tell? Who can I tell? It's awful!" In subsequent primals he relived more of his childhood and youth and for the first time came to accept his previously repressed feelings of anger and rage as normal. His enormous anxiety began to diminish.

After several weeks of daily sessions, clearing his emotional and spiritual nature of forty years of repressed feelings, he joined a Yokefellow group and continued his growth. Previously Jud had been unable to speak in a group or to express himself in any normal social setting. He felt guilty, lonely, and ineffective.

Guilt, of course, was part of his problem — false guilt over legitimate anger toward his sadistic parents. When he could accept those feelings as valid and normal, his healing began. God forgives us freely, but we cannot *feel* forgiven for what we do not confess, and we cannot confess what is buried in the unconscious.

Psychologist Carl Rogers emphasizes the supreme importance of self-acceptance and self-understanding. He maintains that it is virtually impossible for one to understand and accept himself *until someone has accepted him for what he is.* The group's loving acceptance enabled Jud to accept himself for the first time.

Sylvia, a woman in her early fifties, asked for an appointment after a retreat session. She was a quiet, sad woman, radiating depression and hurt. Her hair was so arranged that it was difficult to get a clear picture of what she looked like, for it covered most of her face. She had grown up in extreme poverty. The most significant thing she remembered about her mother was the oft-repeated refrain, "You're the ugliest thing I ever saw. You're just like your father!" There were many more painful details, but that is the one thing I remember most clearly as I think of this middle-aged woman still crippled emotionally by the incessant criticism of her rejecting mother. It was impossible to distinguish her feelings of self-rejection, inferiority, and shame from the emotion of guilt and worthlessness. Her self-hate was enormous and she sensed that it would require long-range therapy to eradicate her lifetime feelings of self-hate.

CAN WE BEAR THE GUILT OF OTHERS?

A person can suffer throughout life for the mistakes of a parent. Julia shared with me at a retreat I was leading that she felt a mixture of negative emotions concerning her father. He had been an inadequate parent, but worse, had ended up in prison with a long sentence to serve. She said, "I find it hard to put my feelings into words. I don't know exactly what it is that I feel. Is it anger? Rage? Disappointment? Hurt? Is it hurt over never having a real father to love me?" She paused for a few moments, then, more or less thinking out loud, said, "For one thing I'm sick to death of bearing my father's guilt! I think I've always felt guilty *for* him, but I'm going to give it up. *I'm* not guilty! *He* is!" She had never been able to put into words before the fact that she felt her father's guilt. Now that she had identified the emotion, she could deal with it. Self-understanding started her on the road to a new level of self-acceptance.

Sometimes a parent, feeling responsible for the way a child turns out, develops a sense of guilt over the failure of the child. Agnes shared in our Yokefellow groups her sense of disappointment and guilt over the fact that her daughter, who had left home, had become a lesbian. She said, "I find it hard even to say the word 'homosexual.' When she comes home at infrequent intervals with her girl friend I can feel only anger and self-pity. Or maybe it's guilt, because I feel I failed her somewhere; but I don't know where."

The group encouraged her to talk out her feelings. No advice was offered, since advice in these groups is considered an insult. Agnes felt greatly relieved when she could share her mixture of emotions with the group.

After a few more sessions, during which she discussed her problem and received the love and support of the group, she reported that she had at last been able to visit her daughter and the girl with whom she lived. She said, "I was able to tell them, sincerely, that I loved them." There was a look of deep satisfaction in her face as she related this.

Without condoning her daughter's way of life, she was giving understanding and love. In the act of expressing love, she felt released from her burden of guilt and self-pity.

There is an admonition in the New Testament that reads, "Confess your sins [hurts, faults, needs] to one another, and pray for one another, that you may be healed" (James 5:16, RSV). Agnes had obeyed this injunction. In sharing her hurt with the group, she was healed of her anger and depression and the guilt that surrounded the entire subject. Since self-love grows out of openness and honesty, Agnes came to have a far better self-image.

SELF-LOVE IS NOT BLUSTER AND ARROGANCE

Sometimes arrogant people give the superficial impression of total self-acceptance. In actuality, they do not like themselves. Their weak self-image is concealed beneath an aggressive facade. They have learned how to fake it. Occasionally, people with low self-esteem tend to admire these arrogant pretenders because they seem so self-assured, so confident, so utterly without self-doubt; but underneath their cloak of pretense they are usually insecure persons who have learned to cover up their sense of inadequacy and self-rejection with a fake bluster or superficial sophistication.

I recall a church officer whose intimidated wife once urged me never to cross him. "He has an ungovernable temper," she said. "He comes home at night and walks up the driveway looking for something to scream about. He is even angrier if he doesn't find something to complain about. He terrorizes the whole family and keeps us in a constant uproar."

At an informal committee meeting in my office one evening, he got up to look for something on the top of a bookcase. He turned and glared at me. "Who took those drawings I put up here?" I said, "Don't shout at me, my friend; I didn't touch your drawings. Save your shouting for your terrified little family." He crumpled, looked embarrassed, and said meekly, "What was that?" I smiled at him, and he grinned back. He never shouted at me again. He was a paper tiger who had learned how to play the game of uproar and enjoyed watching everyone scamper to avoid his fatuous, fake indignation. Beneath his crusty veneer he was a very insecure man, with vast feelings of inferiority and guilt, both real and false. His brusque exterior was a cover-up for weakness he dared not admit even to himself.

SELF-REJECTION AND DIVORCE

It is not only what happens to a child that is important; it is *how the child perceives it*. A six-year-old girl told a little friend, "My daddy doesn't live with us any more. He left because he doesn't like me." In reality, the divorce had nothing to do with the daughter, whom the father loved dearly. The little girl had simply interpreted his departure as meaning: "Daddy's leaving. I must have done something bad or he wouldn't go. That means that he doesn't like me any more." By placing this meaning on the father's leaving, she lost her sense of self-worth. If daddy didn't love her, how could she love herself?

DAMAGE DONE BY FALSE GUILT

From the adult point of view, a divorce is a painful solution to an otherwise intolerable situation. To the young child it can be utterly devastating. A minister's wife at a retreat mentioned at lunch that she had a terrible migraine headache.

"In-Depth Therapy," I said, "is one way of dealing with primal feelings."

"How do you do it?"

I described it as best I could. She said, "I'd never go through that." I changed the subject. A bit later she said, "I just wouldn't think of doing anything like that. It's too scary." She kept returning to the subject, fearfully but persistently. Finally she asked, "Could one session do any good?" I doubted it, and besides, our time before the next session was short, but I agreed to try.

She and her husband and I went into the adjoining room and locked the door. I said, "There is very little time; we'll have to work fast. I can promise nothing, but we'll try." Then I regressed her from her present age back to early childhood and told her that she would find herself in some time and place where she was lonely and frightened. I had her start pounding on some pillows and do the required breathing. She began to cry in the voice of a little girl.

"Where are you?" I asked.

"Under the bed." Still weeping.

"Why are you under the bed?"

"I'm scared." More hysterical weeping.

"Why are you scared?"

"They're fighting. Daddy's going to leave!"

"What will happen if daddy leaves?"

There was a long pause, punctuated by anguished sobs. "I will die!" she said. Her husband and I stood by while she relived the entire traumatic scene, then we held her as her sobs became fainter.

She reported that her headache was gone. I said, "Great! I can't promise that it won't return, because I don't know whether in that brief primal experience we got up all the roots. I'm sure there's much more down there." She said, "Perhaps, but I am very grateful for having been able to get up even that much. Reliving it is vastly different from remembering the event, isn't it?" It is the difference, really, between seeing a picture of a distant scene or being there in person.

Parents and others sometimes unwittingly create situations in which a child can be marred for life. A woman told me that as a child of six or seven she was told that her mother was in very poor health and might die at any time. She was cautioned to take as much of the burden off mother as she could, to enable her to live a long time.

"So," related the woman, "mother complained her way through my childhood, adolescence, and adulthood. She is still living at the age of ninety-one and will probably live to be a hundred. But if she had died when I was little, I am confident I would have felt responsible for her death. It would have been because of something I did or didn't do."

REAL GUILT

But it is not only the false guilt others dump on us. There is the real guilt for which we must take responsibility. Whenever we violate our integrity; anytime we do something contrary to our ethical or moral code, or fail to do what we believe we are supposed to do, we set in motion the incredibly complex guilt syndrome. I term it a "syndrome," because it has many facets and manifestations.

The inner judicial system knows only two verdicts: guilty or innocent. It knows no gray areas. It is inexorable. And once it has announced its verdict, it proceeds to execute justice. If the inner judicial system finds us guilty, it offers two options: either we must confess and accept forgiveness or we must be punished.

It is not God who is speaking, but that portion of us that is called by such names as Conscience, Judicial System, Super Ego, the Inner Self. This part of the self is not necessarily the voice of God, for conscience is largely the product of our parents, our particular environment and culture.

Once the conscience has pronounced us guilty and declared that we must either be forgiven — by God and by ourselves — or be punished, it accept no rationalizations. This portion of the self cannot be deluded, wheedled, or bought off. It accepts no excuses.

If we seek to make things right — by making restitution, asking pardon from God and man, or whatever else may be required — the conscience is satisfied. If for some reason we cannot get a feeling of being forgiven, or if we refuse to alter our guilty conduct, the verdict is pronounced: *you must be punished.* And what a relentless and inexorable part of the personality this is!

Depending on one's type of personality, the verdict may involve becoming trouble-prone or accident-prone, thus having an accident to "pay the price of our defect," or one may "choose" a physical or emotional symptom.

SELF-HATE

Simon Peter hated himself, and he dissolved into bitter tears of self-recrimination. Only a little while before, he had made staunch affirmations of loyalty, and then he heard himself assert for the third time that he had nothing to do with Jesus of Nazareth. He was "not one of them"; but no sooner had he uttered the denial than he saw Jesus turn and look at him. What was in that look? Reproof? Rebuke? Disappointment? Hurt?

"Peter, I knew you would fail me! You're weak, Peter. You've demonstrated that over and over. Why did I ever choose such an undependable person as you for a disciple? All the others have fled, and you followed me here to the trial, but now you — my last hope — have failed me."

No, nothing like that was intended to be conveyed in that glance. We know this by the amazingly tender way Jesus dealt with Simon Peter after the Resurrection. There was no direct reference to his denial, only a request for a threefold affirmation of love, to counterbalance the threefold denial.

But Peter must have read into that glance all sorts of things. He would have projected his own self-contempt and self-hatred onto Jesus, and imagined the sternest rebuke. At any rate, he "went out, and wept bitterly" (Matthew 26:75). Those were tears of remorse and self-loathing for his weakness.

I love Simon Peter. He is so like one of us; like someone I've known in the past and forgotten just when or where. He's familiar. Yes, now I've got it! He's like — not one of us — he's like me! No wonder I felt I'd known him. And if Jesus could treat him with such exquisite tenderness afterward, it tells me how I am going to be received, despite ten thousand failures and blunders.

I feel so sorry for the religious legalists who battered me as a child with a thousand fearful threats. I do not know who warped them; but it has been going on a long time, this matter of making God a vengeful Being to be feared, rather than a loving heavenly Father, who is like Jesus in his tender love for the wayward.

Someone defined a fundamentalist as "a person who is inexpressibly saddened by the knowledge that somewhere, somehow, someone is having a good time!" Those were the people of my childhood.

An ancient Persian text contains this gem: "There is no saint without a past — no sinner without a future." That would make a very suitable epitaph for Simon Peter — or you, or me.

GOD'S LOVE IS MEDIATED THROUGH PERSONS

Myra spent over forty years as a highly effective social worker, retiring at sixty-five. I saw her in counseling sessions over a period of several years before and after her retirement. She had experienced terrible headaches and depression for many years. Medical science provided no answer.

She was a splendid Christian and attended church faithfully. Her church relationships were helpful, but nothing seemed to alleviate the terrible depression and constant pain.

Some well-meaning Christian friends urged her to "just turn it all over to the Lord," and "lay all your burdens at the foot of the cross." Those and other clichés served to make her feel all the more frustrated, for she was doing everything she could to "believe" and to "trust."

Her mother had died when she was two, after a long illness. "My father was a fine man, but he never expressed any emotion," she said. "I sensed early in life that there was nothing in life for me, and there hasn't been anything except a lifetime of depression. I hurt all the time, and it never gets any better."

There had been no surrogate mother to hold and cuddle her, no one to give her love and warmth. Never having been loved, she did not know how to give or receive love, though she desperately longed to. Wanting, needing, and fearing men, she never married, but often spoke longingly of her desire to have a home and family. "I feel that I've never lived," she said. "I've never known what to do with my life, and now that I am retired, though I have undertaken volunteer work, nothing gives me any satisfaction."

Myra — and millions like her — constitute a living refutation of the idea that life is simple, that all you have to do is "believe," and life thereafter will be radiantly beautiful and without pain. Jesus did not find it so on the cross, nor did the disciples who were imprisoned and executed. The apostle Paul, not noted as a complainer, gives a heartbreaking account of some of the hardships he had endured. Far from giving us a simplistic, rosy-hued picture of life, Jesus affirms that "In the world you have tribulation" (John 16:33, RSV).

I do not profess to know the whole answer to sin, suffering, and sorrow, but we know how it will turn out, when "the kingdom of the world has become the kingdom of our Lord and of his Christ" (Revelation 11:15, RSV).

It is not promised that we will stop hurting when we are converted, but we are commanded *to love one another*, so that hurts like Myra's can be prevented. For "love is the medicine for the healing of the world."[1]

GUILT — INDECISION AND INCOMPATIBLE GOALS

Guilt, at its core, is *trying to pursue incompatible goals*. Thus, the inner self is split, wanting two conflicting things and unable to achieve this impossible goal.

The emotion known as guilt functions basically like an alarm clock. When the alarm goes off, it has served its purpose and the awakened person normally turns it off. The alarm is "good" in that it alerts one to the fact that it is time to get up. It feels "bad" in that it awakens one from a sound sleep.

In daily life when we violate our principles, the warning signal called "guilt" alerts us. We can feel a vague, gnawing sense of remorse, or uneasiness, or anxiety. This disquiet will continue until we have rectified the error and receive forgiveness. Then the feeling should dissipate. *Half an hour is long enough to feel guilty about anything, once the issue has been resolved through repentance.* Hopefully, one will examine the matter to make sure that it is not repeated.

It is not an irate God who is condemning us and making us feel uneasy and remorseful. It is the inner judicial system, which is much stronger in some people than in others. John Bunyan found great difficulty in feeling forgiven for having rung the church bell as a boyish prank. Other people commit serious crimes with less compunction. Conscience can be a vengeful, inexorable, vindictive foe if one was reared in an authoritative and punitive environment. Or, it can be so weak that, like a defective alarm clock, it gives only a mild tinkle or none at all.

You like yourself better when you have done what you feel you *should* have done, whether it involves paying all of your income tax, taking out the garbage, or visiting a sick friend. Failure to "do right" always registers as guilt, and you lose self-worth. You like yourself less well; then it becomes difficult, if not impossible, to love yourself. How can you learn to like or love a self that consistently fails to do the right thing?

Sin Erodes Self-Esteem

In the matter of sins of commission, if you find yourself, through weakness or intent, doing something out of harmony with your own moral code, somewhere within you court has convened; the inner judge has seated himself on the bench; witnesses (in the form of thoughts, promises, commitments, memories) are called, and the trial begins. The trial moves with astonishing rapidity, unlike those trials where opposing attorneys rise every few minutes to raise objections.

This judicial system (conscience) is set up by God, not because he is unloving or vindictive, but because he loves us and wants us to live without inner conflict. He is anxious for us to live in harmony with a matchless set of universal principles that he established for our happiness and well-being.

Jesus said, "Now you know this truth; how happy you will be if you put it into practice" (John 13:17, TEV). He was making it clear that our happiness and well-being are inexorably linked up with obeying the universal principles he had been teaching. To expect God's blessings and guidance without seeking to follow his formula would be as futile as asking God to "make it a good cake, Lord," after we had failed to follow the recipe; or invoking his help in getting a car started without turning on the ignition.

This is not a capricious universe. It operates on unalterable principles, as much so in the spiritual realm as in the realm of physics or biology.

The traffic judge who fines us for going through a red light is not being unreasonable or vindictive. He is trying to remind us to be more careful, for our own sake and that of others. In the same spirit, our inner judge is anxious to guard our individual safety and well-being and the safety and well-being of those around us.

The inner judge, or conscience, is not an enemy, but our friend. He is on our side, no matter how often we may fail. His ultimate goal is to help us avoid all actions or attitudes that prevent us from loving ourselves properly. Conscience is not God, but his agent. Thus your inner judicial system seeks your safety and wholeness and well-being, just as our legal system functions to preserve the well-being of our society.

Some judges tend to be lenient; some, more severe. There are people whose inner judicial systems are overly strict and punitive; others have too lenient and lackadaisical a conscience. A discerning friend, pastor, or counselor can help you discover whether your conscience is overly strict or underdeveloped.

One thing is very clear: you can never love yourself properly as long as you violate divine principles. Obey your inner voice, and you will respect yourself. Ignore it, and you will despise yourself.

Notes

[1]Karl Menninger, *Love Against Hate* (New York: Harcourt Brace Jovanovich, 1959).

4 How to Tell If You Lack a Proper Self-Love

4 How to Tell If You Lack a Proper Self-Love

> Oftimes nothing profits more than self-esteem
> Grounded on just and right
> Well managed.
>
> — *John Milton*

The key word in this chapter is *excessive*. For instance, everyone is capable of being irritated at times. *Excessive* irritability suggests some degree of neurosis, a malfunctioning of the personality.

Here is a check list to enable you to discover whether, or to what degree, you lack self-love. (A brief psychological test to check on your degree of self-acceptance and self-love will be found in Appendix C.)

1. *Are you considered overly sensitive by friends or family?*

Most normal people have their feelings hurt on occasion. Few persons are totally immune to rejection or insult. The acid test is: Are you more easily offended than most people? Does it require a long time for you to recover from a hurt?

2. *Are you argumentative?*

Some people feel an overwhelming urge to argue. They have an excessive need to prove their point. The ancient truth still applies: "A man convinced against his will is of the same opinion still."

Individuals with a weak sense of identity, if they happen to have aggressive temperaments, can seldom resist the temptation to debate any and all issues. They get involved in futile arguments about politics, religion (two subjects always best avoided where strong difference of opinion exists), books, morals, movies, TV shows, child rearing, or whatever they have strong feelings about.

When I was much younger, I frequently succumbed to the temptation to show people where they were wrong. In one such encounter a very wise old man said, smiling, "In matters of taste there can be no argument." That slowed me down. Whether it be taste in manners, religion, literature, politics, art, or food, there is no point in arguing about a matter where one person's opinion may be quite as valid as that of another. An amiable discussion is quite another matter.

3. *Are you a critical person?*

An excessively critical attitude is a dead giveaway. It reveals an individual who has a very poor opinion of himself. The worst critic is usually the one who is unconsciously most critical of himself. He dislikes himself intensely and when he gets fed up with his own self-hate, he projects the rest onto those about him in the form of criticism. While striving to gain a greater degree of self-esteem, it is wise to stifle the impulse to be critical. It is more than a bad habit, for its roots go deep into one's self-rejections; but it *is* a habit, and it can be broken. Form the habit of focusing on the positive. Others will like you better and that will enable you to like yourself better.

Many years ago I invited a highly qualified man to make a presentation to my board, with the hope that they would engage him for a specific and — to me — much-needed financial campaign. After a two-hour presentation and discussion the board voted the idea down. I was deeply disappointed.

As I drove the man to the airport, I vented my criticism of the board. I voiced it strongly. In fact, I was disgusted with their short-sightedness. In the midst of my tirade the man laid his hand on my arm lightly and said, "Let me tell you about my children." What a gentle but powerful rebuke! I have never forgotten his kindly message.

4. *Are you intolerant of others? Of their ideas?*

People who are intolerant of other races, religions, ideas, or concepts, are broadcasting loud and clear: "I am a hostile, self-rejecting individual."

Gabriel Montalban once said, "There are a thousand shades

of gray." As there are many colors and shades in the spectrum, so there is room for a wide variety of temperaments. It might simplify things if everyone thought as I do, and agreed with me, and liked what I like. But we are all uniquely different, just as every snowflake that ever fell to earth has a different pattern. God seems to dislike exact duplicates.

Yet, most of us at times are puzzled, or even angered, that other people can feel and think so differently. It seems a bit strange to me that some people eat snails, that many businessmen in the Middle East sit around a good part of the day smoking hubble-bubble pipes, that Eskimos eat blubber, that millions of people flock daily to cocktail bars and talk trivia. New Year's Eve celebrations strike me as ridiculous, chiefly because I dislike crowds.

Extreme left-wingers and rabid right-wingers appall me. Why can't they be well balanced like I am, a staunch progressive, anxious to preserve the values of the past but willing to explore new methods and ideas? All extremists puzzle or frighten me.

Why can't men wear their hair like mine? And dress as I do? Why do young people affect that ridiculous, outlandish, sloppy attire?

But hold on a minute! Why shouldn't people eat snails, or snakes for that matter? I am told that rattlesnake meat tastes very much like chicken. As for the hubble-bubble pipe smokers, if they find life more pleasant that way, who am I, a mere compulsive worker, to object to their life style? Eskimos, I hear, need fat for metabolic purposes. The avid party-goers simply rate higher on social need than I do. And why should it bother me that people want to whoop it up on New Year's Eve? Why can't I let them do their thing? As for the left- and right-wingers, I now recall having led a wildcat strike at a Detroit automobile plant in my youth — and got fired for my radicalism. I'd forgotten about that. The political extremists are exercising their constitutional rights. Why should that bother me excessively?

And hair styles and matters of dress? My distaste for styles and ideas divergent from mine tells me that I am really asking, "Why can't people be more like me?" That's a pretty egotistical stance, now that I come to think of it.

5. *Are you an excessively angry person?*

Do you "blow up" easily? Anger is not evil. It is a God-instilled survival emotion. All human emotions are divine in origin, given to us for our protection. God wants us to survive.

What *is* evil is the misuse of anger. We have a right to our feelings. Children should never be punished for expressing their emotions. They should be guided as to when and where to express them.

If you want to make a more extended study of anger in the Bible, I urge you to read Psalms 18:37-42; 21:10; 109; 137:8,9.

Psalm 109 is one of David's most vitriolic. In it he expresses violent, murderous anger. He is in a towering rage that leaves no room for compassion or reasonableness. The Bible does not include this masterpiece of invective as an example of how we are to treat people. Rather, it is an excellent example of how to dump one's anger in a way that will not be destructive to others. David obviously wrote this trembling with rage. You can practice this too. When you are outraged, go to your room and express your rage. Talk it out. Shout and scream if you feel like it. Don't sound nice and pious. Be real! All emotions are valid.

Then write a letter, just as David wrote out his feelings. Tell the offender off! Make it strong. Don't mince words. Forget all about tact and reasonableness. But having written it, don't mail it, of course! Just let it lie there for a few days. Read it again later, and smile at the blind rage you felt. You will never forget the relief experienced by expressing your honest feelings.

The key is this: We have a right to our anger, but we do not have the right to dump our hostility on other people and crush them. Jesus got angry on more than one occasion. Everyone remembers how he cleansed the temple with flaming indignation. On another occasion he "looked around at [the Pharisees] with anger, grieved at their hardness of heart . . ." (Mark 3:5, RSV). Notice the difference, however, between his anger and ours; Jesus was angry over the desecration of the temple, and at the Pharisees because they lacked compassion for a crippled man. We usually get most angry when we have been insulted or abused in some way. With us it is usually a personal thing; Jesus seemed never to be angry over personal insults.

The more passive person accepts criticism or abuse, feels that he cannot express his hurt, and turns it inward. His subsequent depression is the result of what is termed "inwardly directed hostility." He has buried his anger. It doesn't go away; it is transmuted into depression or a physical symptom. The aggressive individual who has been offended tends to erupt and feels justified in attacking the object of his wrath. Others, neither very passive nor aggressive, may alternate between turning their anger inward occasionally and expressing it in some way.

6. *Are you forgiving?*

Some years ago I spent a few hours with a relative who was then around ninety. I had not seen him for many years and remembered him as an exceptionally hostile person. Now I saw that age had eroded his explosive nature somewhat. He appeared much calmer. Sometimes the approaching of the Angel of Death does instill in one a greater capacity for gentleness.

But as he reminisced he showed some of his old spirit. Relating something that had happened sixty years before in a small town in Texas, he grew more and more tense, then hostile, and finally bitter. I could see that he still had traces of the old unforgiving spirit that had marked him when he was younger. Sixty years seems a long time to carry a grudge.

Those who do not love themselves have a weak self-image, and it is often very difficult for them to forgive. It is as though they would lose something precious were they to extend the olive branch. Lacking the "glue" of self-respect and a proper self-love to hold the personality together, they use the adhesive of old hates and grudges. Though they are usually unaware of the process, it goes like this: "I cannot forgive myself; thus I cannot forgive anyone else."

The unforgiving person does irreparable harm to his personality. The human organism functions far better when there is a sense of "being at peace." When a grudge is held, there can be no serenity. The grudge creates stress, and continued stress is destructive of the organism. Excessive, continued stress paves the way for a host of physical symptoms: ulcers, heart attacks, asthma, neurodermatitis (a severe skin condition that seldom yields to medication), migraine headaches, colitis, rheumatoid arthritis, and many others. This is not to say that repressed hostility alone causes such symptoms, but it is usually a component. So, Jesus suggests that when you are worshiping and suddenly recall that *someone has something against you* (any impaired relationship), leave the worship service and seek out the offended or offending person (Matthew 5:24.) Make it right to the best of your ability is the admonition of Jesus. Then return and go on with your worship.

The message is clear: We cannot pray or worship effectively, nor meet the conditions for receiving God's blessings if we are spiritually and emotionally out of harmony, filled with stress and conflict created by impaired relationships. We cannot love ourselves properly when we are unforgiving. We are out of synchronization with God's beautiful cosmic harmony that seeks to bless and guide us.

7. *Are you excessively jealous?*

The word excessive is used here, since everyone is, to some degree, capable of jealousy.[1] Possessiveness and jealousy usually go together. They are often the product of childhood experiences or influences, rendering the individual very insecure.

A couple seeing me about their marriage came to the point quickly. She complained of his terrible jealousy and possessiveness. He would scarcely let her out of his sight and even insisted on going shopping with her, lest she flirt with someone in the store. She admitted that before they were married she enjoyed evidences of his possessiveness, which she mistook for love. Now it was driving her out of her mind.

His mother had been seriously ill for several years while he was very young. Later she had been "taken away," as he put it, by death. I explained that his extreme possessiveness was a natural outgrowth of childhood feelings about the loss of his mother; thus, he felt a need to "hang on" to his wife lest she be "taken away" like his mother.

But of course this type of neurosis is not affected by advice or explanation. Only long-range therapy can provide a solution. It is difficult, but not impossible, to eradicate an anxiety neurosis rooted in childhood.

Though everyone is capable of jealousy in some degree, it is only when it becomes excessive that it interferes seriously with relationships or one's peace of mind. Pathological jealousy and possessiveness place too much of a burden on a relationship. One husband, whose wife could not endure for him to be out of her sight except during working hours, finally said to her, "I don't know the source of your problem, but your possessiveness is killing me, and I have no intention of putting up with it indefinitely. You can either get some professional help or I will want a divorce. This is not a threat but an honest feeling."

She came to me for counseling, and we quickly discovered that her jealousy related to her father, who had disappeared when she was a little girl. She had been fearful and insecure ever since. In time, her deep insecurity yielded to In-Depth Therapy.

If you find yourself inordinately jealous or possessive, you can be sure that you lack self-love. One with such deep insecurities finds it very difficult to develop a proper self-esteem.

Intensive therapy is usually indicated, not simplistic advice or positive thinking.[2]

8. *Are you a poor listener?*

    I once had a friend who had a remarkable store of jokes, which he told well. He was a splendid public speaker and used his stories and jokes to excellent advantage. But he was never known to laugh, or even smile, at jokes told by anyone else. When he was the center of attention his eyes sparkled. When the conversation veered away from him, his eyes glazed over. He was a good speaker, but a poor listener.

    Such a person is so preoccupied with his own feelings and his own self-importance that he simply cannot bring himself to listen to anyone else. He is in short, a self-centered, not a self-loving person. One who is at peace with himself can forget himself part of the time. If you accept yourself, like yourself, believe in yourself, you can endure having the conversation include others, and listen with interest.

    Someone reported, "I used to respond to most things people said with 'Baloney,' and I had very few friends. Then I changed, and began to say 'Marvelous,' and now I'm invited everywhere." His semifacetious comment contains more than a grain of truth.

    The appreciative listener, though he may have to "fake" it until it becomes a habit, is exhibiting an important trait. In time, he will come to like himself better, because listening can be an act of love; and we always like ourselves better when we act in love.

9. *Are you excessively materialistic? Do you have a poverty complex?*

    There is always a perfectly valid explanation for any neurosis.[3] When I discover the childhood source of a person's neurosis, I invariably find myself feeling understanding, concern, and compassion. But the world at large is not going to take the time to try to understand the origin of our neurotic behavior patterns. If you have a poverty complex, it will seem the most rational thing in the world to you. I have a friend who has his garage, two rooms of his home, the patio, the shed, and part of the yard, piled high with what I would call junk. To him it has enormous value: "I might need that someday," he tells his patient but frustrated wife. He has accumulated this amazing collection of mechanical and electrical junk through the years. He can justify each piece, must of which rusts or rots long before he has an opportunity to catalog it, much less use it. He experienced poverty and emotional deprivation in childhood, though not more than millions of other children. In addition, there was a mentally unstable mother and an absentee father. The combination caused his insecurity to take the form of a pack-rat complex.

I have a mild poverty complex and am a collector. I collect ancient artifacts, such as Roman glassware, amphora from the Aegean Sea, pottery from two to four thousand years old, and the like. I would like to believe that this is rooted solely in a love of beauty and ancient civilizations, but I am aware that this is only partly true. It originates in a mild insecurity. Like all complexes, this originated in childhood. I recall hearing my mother say in a manner that irritated me even at age four: "No, we can't afford that." For some reason I translated that to mean "We're poor," and believed it for years, though it was never true.

A true miser, or a person with a full-blown poverty complex, saves ridiculous things for absurd reasons, and the degree of the hang-up is the measure of the insecurity lurking in that person's personality. Insecurity is based on fear; and one with a great deal of fear usually has comparatively little self-love.

One who truly loves himself can have wealth without pride, or poverty without humiliation. He is fundamentally "nonattached." He takes neither life nor himself too seriously. His center is in himself, rather than in persons or things. He can rejoice in beauty and possessions, or lose them without loss of serenity. In loving God, his neighbor, and himself, his basic needs are met, because all things of value flow out of that triangular love affair with God, others, and self.

10. *Are you greatly impressed by titles, degrees, honors, badges?*

There is nothing fundamentally wrong with titles, degrees, and honors. They become deterrents to emotional and spiritual growth only when one values them excessively.

If, without too much struggle or at too great a sacrifice, one is able to win some honors or certificates or blue ribbons, or if society insists on bestowing them, fine. But the tense preoccupation with status symbols is something else. One who fully accepts himself and loves himself properly, can be happy without certification by others; but if honors are awarded, he can accept them graciously and value them for what they are: mild expressions of appreciation, or evidence of success in pursuit of some significant goal. They would mean something to him, but he would not overvalue them.

I, who was very grateful for having an honorary degree

awarded me many years ago, like to think what Jesus might have said had some prestigious institution offered him such an honor. My private conviction is that he would undoubtedly have smiled, waved his arm toward that mixed rabble following him, and said something like, "These are my prizes, my awards. I have no greater need than that they love me, obey me, and follow me."

At the present state of our spiritual development most of us probably need our badges, titles, degrees, and certificates of merit. I do not deprecate them. I simply suggest that they be viewed as props for sagging egos, to keep us going until we can gain a greater degree of self-love.

11. *Are you a poor loser?*

Phillip is a highly successful surgeon. He is personable, cheerful, nice-looking, and appears to be a well-integrated personality. One glaring symptom that turned up in his counseling sessions was the fact that he is one of the world's worst losers.

In fact, he *never loses.* If necessary, he cheats in order to win the game. Worse still, even playing games with his own children — checkers, croquet, or touch football — he consistently cheats, or will insist on playing "just one more game" until he can win.

Here is blatant evidence of a weak ego. Although he has achieved significantly as an adult, his childhood was marked by so much rejection that he feels not quite acceptable either to himself or to others. "Losing" represents a loss of self-esteem to him.

People who easily lose their tempers in playing games — or in an argument, for that matter — reveal something important about themselves: *They do not like themselves.* Aggressive self-haters will fight, argue, contend, or even cheat to win; more passive self-haters tend more often to go into depression, or at least become moody, a manifestation of mild depression.

12. *Do you find it hard to accept compliments?*

According to a study conducted at Colorado State University, two out of three people feel uncomfortable when paid a compliment.[4] Half of the 245 subjects surveyed felt obligated to return the compliments or reciprocate in some fashion. Thirty percent felt they would appear conceited if they failed to neutralize the compliments gracefully, and twenty percent suspected that ulterior motives lay behind the praise.

"Compliments often give rise to uneasiness, defensiveness,

and cynicism," according to Professor Ronny Turner, who conducted the survey. There was a tendency, upon receiving a verbal compliment, to say, "Oh, you say such nice things"; "I had lots of help"; "It was really nothing"; "It would have been better if . . ."; "I was lucky"; or wait for the compliments to be followed by criticism. Other typical responses from the majority were, "I can't take all the credit"; "Anyone could have done it"; "This old thing? I've had it for years."

There is a basic psychological law to this effect: We tend to act in harmony with our self-image. If our self-image (self-respect, self-love, self-worth) is weak, a compliment may be out of harmony with the way we perceive ourselves, in which case we tend to reject it.

What *can* one say, then, that does not seem conceited, nor yet self-abasing? Self-accepting people respond with neither "Oh, I thought my performance was awful!" or "Yes, I agree I was pretty wonderful." Instead, a simple "Thank you" suffices. By practicing that, one can overcome any mild embarrassment when praise is offered.

SELF-LOVE AND ONE'S HEALTH

A young woman had been seeing me in private sessions for quite some time and was also in a therapy group. Her anxiety was almost unbelievable. She was able to hold down a job, but when the day was over, she was, as she expressed it, "a basket case." The group experience did not seem to help. Eventually I said, "I want you to see a physician friend of mine for a six-hour glucose tolerance test. I think it probable that you have hypoglycemia" (low blood sugar). She resisted strongly, until I refused to see her unless she would have the test.

The results revealed that she was severely hypoglycemic. She was put on a low-blood-sugar diet (high protein, low carbohydrate). Within a few weeks, her excessive anxiety had vanished. She began to react normally. No one is able to say for sure whether emotional stress is the cause of the malfunctioning organism or whether it is the physical symptom that produces the emotional distress. Perhaps it really doesn't matter.

Another young woman who I felt might have the same problem returned with the diagnosis of diabetes.

A middle-aged man with a very weak self-image went through several years of intensive therapy with half a dozen different therapists in an effort to get some relief. Eventually, he had extensive In-Depth Therapy with significant results. However, there was still something missing. I sent him in for blood tests, specifying particularly the test for hypoglycemia. He, too, was suffering from low blood sugar. A month on the new diet did nothing for him. Then, after five weeks he began to feel much better. To his great satisfaction, he eventually lost forty pounds, and his inner tension continued to lessen. What I am saying at this point is that there is no one simple solution. I wish there were. A thousand and one things can go wrong with the human organism, intensifying the result of an already weak self-image.

Sigmund Freud wrote to a friend in 1927: "I am firmly convinced that one day all these disturbances we are trying to understand will be treated by means of hormones or similar substances." This was before the discovery of vitamins and prior to the improvement of many modern medical techniques. Hopefully, in the next few decades new medical discoveries will make possible the alleviation of many emotional and physical ailments that are so baffling at the present time.

WHY MUST WE SUFFER?

Why should it have to be this way? Why must we be marred? Why should this have to happen to us? I have heard these anguished questions again and again. A partial answer is that these deficiencies are equivalent to the net we put up across the tennis court. There is no game *unless we make it difficult.* It would be easier to get the ball into the other court if there were no net there. But we insist on putting handicaps into the games we invent for ourselves. There is no contest, no game, without the sand trap, the tennis net, the penalties. And so it is with life. Not having had perfect parents or peers or siblings is the equivalent of the tennis net. The goal is to get the ball over the net as often as possible. You don't have to win, but you have to keep on playing.

On my desk is a printed card that every counselee ultimately looks at. A man in an explorer's helmet is frantically pursuing with a net a very elusive butterfly. The caption is: "Nobody ever said it was going to be easy!"

Notes

[1]In his *Dictionary of Psychoanalysis*, ed. Nandor Fodor and Frank Gaynor (New York: Fawcett Publications, Inc., 1958), Sigmund Freud writes, "Jealousy

is one of those affective states, like grief, that may be described as normal. If anyone appears to be without it, the inference is justified that it has undergone severe repression and consequently plays all the greater part in his unconscious mental life. . . . The three stages of jealousy may be described as (1) competitive or normal, (2) projected, (3) delusional jealousy."

[2]This is not to disparage positive thinking, which can be very helpful at times, but deep neurotic behavior patterns normally require more intensive therapy.

[3]*Neurosis* is a catch-all term with many definitions, perhaps the simplest of which is: a strong to severe overreaction.

[4]*Newsweek*, August 4, 1975.

5 What Self-Love Is Not

5 What Self-Love Is Not

> What a man thinks of himself . . . determines his fate.
>
> — *Henry David Thoreau*

Although the terms *self-love, self-acceptance, self-esteem,* and *self-approval* are not precisely synonymous, there is a sense in which we can use them interchangeably. For our purposes in this chapter we can refer to self-accepting people as those who love themselves.

1. *The self-accepting person is not driven by neurotic ambition.*

A psychiatric dictionary defines ambition as "a defense against shame." It is the shame of being or feeling inferior to others. This does not disparage the legitimate desire to attain some worthwhile goal.

Visiting one day with an elderly relative whose raging ambition had destroyed her health and her marriage and then forced her to spend thirty years in bed suffering from psychosomatic ailments, I recalled a conversation we had when I was sixteen. I had just announced to the family my intention of entering the ministry. Little in my past performance or attitudes gave any hint that I was at all qualified. My father could not suppress a cynical smile of disbelief.

Later my superambitious relative took me aside and said earnestly, "If you are going to enter the ministry, I want you to become a second George W. Truett." At that time Dr. Truett was the pastor of the largest Protestant church in the world, and an orator of wide renown. I recall saying, "No, I don't want to become a second George W. Truett. I want to become a first Cecil Osborne." She was grievously disappointed.

An excessive drive to excel, to win over others, to stand out, to be superior, to be the richest, the most powerful, to have the most of something, springs not from a proper self-love, but often from a deep sense of inferiority.

Alfred Adler, one of Freud's early disciples, came to feel that the basic human urge was not the sex drive, as Freud had postulated, but the drive to excel, to overcome one's feelings of weakness and helplessness; in short, to compensate for feelings of inferiority.

Competitiveness has its place, particularly in games and sports, but emotionally mature people learn to compete only with their previous best, not with others. (Someone has pointed out that the world's best swordsman has nothing to fear from the world's second best swordsman, but he had better flee in haste from an angry farmer with a pitchfork.) One should compete, if at all, in his own field, and with the awareness that others may be more greatly endowed.

Personally, I don't want to compete with anyone, in any realm. If I were to compete with someone, I might discover that his natural endowments are less than mine, and my goal would therefore be too low; or his abilities may far outstrip mine, and I could become discouraged.

True self-esteem can give one the quiet determination to surpass his previous performance. That might involve anything from trying to win two blue ribbons instead of the one received last year, or to decide to live life more fully than heretofore.

Jesus found the competitive spirit operating in the Twelve on more than one occasion. There was the time James and John asked to be given prestigious positions when Jesus came into his kingdom (Matthew 20:20-28). The other disciples were angry about this, and one presumes it was partly because they would have loved such honors themselves (Luke 22:24-27).

At the Last Supper Jesus laid aside his outer robe, took a towel and basin, and proceeded to wash the disciples' feet, in the role of a servant. In this quiet demonstration of humility he rebuked their contentious rivalry (John 13:3-11).

Jesus once asked an enigmatic question, a text seldom used

as the basis for sermons: "How can you believe, who receive glory from one another?" (John 5:44, RSV). The clear implication is that the seeking of honors and distinctions is incompatible with developing a deep faith.

2. *One who has self-esteem is not overcompliant.*

The excessively compliant individual has the unconscious goal of winning love and approval from *everyone*. Such a person finds it almost impossible to say no. This tendency usually originates early in childhood, as the result of a need to win parental love when the child has some reason to doubt that love.

How People Become Overcompliant

Kathy was reliving a buried memory from her earliest childhood during an In-Depth counseling session. She experienced herself seated on the floor playing while her mother and a neighbor were talking. She heard her mother say, "I didn't want a fourth child. This kid has been crying ever since she was born. I really didn't *need* another child." Kathy, talking not *about* her mother but *to* her, screamed, "Mommy, mommy, don't say that! Don't say that! I'll be good; I'll do *anything, anything,* if you won't ever say that again!" Kathy wept for half an hour over the agonizing realization that she was not wanted. As a child she never cried again, and became totally compliant, not only with her mother *but with everyone else.* She said later, "I know now, for the first time, why I have never been able to say no to anyone. In reliving that experience I felt myself making a lifetime vow to give in and do whatever mommy or anyone else wanted, if only they would love me." With this insight Kathy also discovered why she had been sexually permissive. People who cannot say no are usually overcommitted, because of their great need to accede to every request. They often feel rushed and hectic and complain of being terribly busy. Their weak sense of identity is excessively dependent upon feeling needed.

Kathy embarked on a course of learning to say no when it was appropriate. I told her that at first it would be very difficult, and that she might find it easier initially to reply, "Yes, I'd be glad to [giving herself time to think], but I won't be able to fit it into my schedule." This avoided the use of the self-forbidden "no," and allowed her the right to refuse when it seemed appropriate.

A delightful friend of mine, a minister, said ruefully, "I have character by consensus. I invariably have to find out what other people think, or feel, and then I always agree with them. I hate myself for it!" Undoubtedly, if he were to search in the primal feelings not accessible to the conscious mind, he would find, as Kathy did, that he had made a similar vow to be supercompliant.

Many people of outstanding ability, as the result of childhood conditioning, have been rendered overcompliant. Charles Darwin was so fearful of his father's disapproval that he delayed twenty-six years before publishing his world-shaking theory of organic evolution.

3. *One with self-esteem is not easily defeated.*
   History records the case of

> a shiftless, rolling stone of a husband married to an illegitimate girl from the Virginia mountains. He tried five or six farms and kept moving on, a man afflicted, we'd say today, with a character neurosis, who thought that by picking a new place, like a movie actress who keeps picking a new husband, he would somehow change the plot. He didn't of course.
>
> They plodded into Indiana, and did a little better. In time, they had a barn and a few animals, a little corral, a rail fence, and they planted corn and flax and beans. But then the neighbors came down with the 'milk sickness,' picked up from cows that chewed on snakeroot. Our farmer's wife died. So the vagabond father and son moved on to a new state and new ground, the son passing from an almost animal boyhood into a bleak manhood; yet out of that frail woman and her listless husband and the poorest ground, there came something strange and wholly admirable: the slow-moving son who seized a Republic and held it through its first cataclysm — Abraham Lincoln.[1]

And of course everyone is familiar with the innumerable setbacks he suffered before becoming president — a business failure that saddled him with the debts of a dishonest partner; failure after failure as he sought public office; but some subtle combination of will, determination, and innate, homespun wisdom and intelligence, and a character rooted and grounded in a simple faith in God, provided him with sufficient self-esteem and inner strength to triumph over every obstacle.

WINNING WITHOUT LOVE

How can we account for these bruised and battered children of misfortune and hardship who, in defiance of all laws of probability, succeed in reaching their goals? Bob is a delightful, humorous young man in his early thirties whom I have come to know and admire. His father is a half-breed Crow, his mother a half-breed Cherokee. They met on the reservation. The grandparents with eleven children had been moved from an Indian reservation to the West Coast in a boxcar. Two children died of dysentery on the way.

Bob grew up on the West Coast among lumber people. "My nickname was 'Worthless.' I'd do anything, no matter how demeaning just to get a few positive strokes," he said. When he was nine, he began felling timber with a chain saw. His back was broken twice, his left leg shattered several times, his right leg once, and both arms and eighteen ribs were smashed in logging accidents.

A few months before he was eleven, because he refused to work for an older brother without being paid, his father ordered him out of the house. He went to work for a neighboring farmer for a dollar a day, milking sixteen cows night and morning, together with other chores. He worked there two years, then gravitated to Alaska where he worked on a fishing boat. Entirely on his own, he worked his way through high school.

"I was befriended by the part-time pastor of a local church. He was a very warm, loving, accepting kind of person, and through him I was led to Christ. He encouraged me to continue my education. Eventually I finished college, then went on to seminary." Bob now pastors a growing Baptist church in the Northwest. He says, "Of all the tragedies in my life, the one that weighs the heaviest is the death of my mother-in-law several years ago. My wife came from a very warm, affirming home, and I had developed a close relationship with her parents. It was very rewarding. They became my surrogate parents, of course, taking the place of the ones who utterly rejected me."

Bob still has areas of insecurity, like most people; but he has managed to surmount a host of obstacles. From some inner reservoir he drew strength to survive, and from a loving, concerned minister and his wife's parents he received the love and affirmation that enabled him to continue against all odds.

The general rule is that we learn to love by having been loved in childhood. The deprivation of this love in most instances is terribly damaging to the personality. For reasons not clearly understood as yet, there are people who have a high survival factor, who manage to survive, achieve significantly, and learn to love, despite a wretched start in life. These are self-accepting people who, in accepting themselves as okay, come to believe that they can not only survive, but also learn to give and receive love.

4. *Self-accepting people are not overly sensitive.*

The Bible recognizes that it is normal for humans to have their feelings hurt on occasion. A person so lacking in sensitivity that he is never hurt by personal slights and injuries would not be normal.

The Old Testament recounts a dramatic story involving impetuous young David, a wealthy rancher named Jabal, and his beautiful wife, Abigail. Fleeing from King Saul's jealous wrath, David and six hundred men hid out in the cave of Adullum, in a barren, rocky area a few miles from present-day Bethlehem.

Nearby was the vast acreage owned by a churlish, evil-tempered man named Jabal. David and his men had carefully protected Jabal's flocks from raiders and predators. In serious need of provisions for his men, David sent emissaries to Jabal asking for food. Jabal responded with insolence and insults. When David received the message, he vowed vengeance, declaring that he would destroy every male in the household of Jabal; whereupon he set out with four hundred armed men to carry out his threat.

Learning of his intention, Jabal's wife, Abigail, loaded a convoy of animals with food and went to meet David and his followers. The poignant account of her meeting with David makes fascinating reading. "I accept all the blame in this matter," she said. "Jabal is a bad-tempered boor, but please don't pay attention to what he has to say. He is a fool — just like his name means." Then she asked pardon for her boldness, offered the gift of the food, and pleaded with David not to have murder on his conscience. David was deeply moved by the winsome appeal of this beautiful woman, and replied, "Bless the Lord God of Israel who has sent you to meet me today! Thank God for your good sense! Bless you for keeping me from murdering the man and carrying out vengeance with my own hands . . . if you had not come to meet me, not one of Jabal's men would be alive tomorrow morning" (1 Samuel 25:32-34, *The Living Bible*).

The Bible portrays its heroes with their weaknesses as well as their strengths. It makes no effort to gloss over their defects. Particularly in his youth David was hot-tempered and impetuous. He was easily insulted, and quick to take offense; but he was equally ready to apologize and make amends. We do ourselves and others a great disservice when we imply — or teach — that

Christians will never be angry. Of course we will! Everyone is capable of anger to some degree. We can all be irritated, or frustrated. It is simply a part of our humanity. The Bible does not teach that we will not have these emotions; it simply urges us to control them. If we fail, as we often will, we are to make amends.

GENIUS AND SELF-ACCEPTANCE

A biographer describes Beethoven as so touchy and overly sensitive that he bordered on paranoia. His closest friends were on occasion liable to find themselves excluded because of some imagined slight. He became increasingly morose and suspicious. He lacked the capacity for a sustained relationship with people, and particularly with a woman, though he desired it very much. His enormous aggression was sublimated in his music, or he might have succumbed to some degree of paranoid schizophrenia.

Beethoven was quite well aware of his musical genius and he did not doubt for an instant that he would rank as one of the world's greatest composers; but there is little evidence that he accepted or liked himself as a person.

It seems unfortunate that the gift of genius so often predisposes one toward emotional lopsidedness. One eminent psychologist has suggested that a certain excessiveness is essential to significant achievement; that those who are "too well balanced" emotionally seem to be on dead center. Significant achievement is often purchased at the price of emotional balance. Those whose goal is contentment and inner serenity are willing to forego the pleasure of greater achievement. Though this seems to be the general rule, it cannot be construed as a psychological law.

The apostle Paul, whom some psychologists do not think of as one of the most well-balanced individuals in history despite his enormous contribution to Christianity, appears to have had a very normal capacity to be hurt by criticism.

He had founded the thriving church at Corinth, but after he moved on, a brilliant orator named Apollos became the pastor. The members now compared Paul to this great preacher. They said of Paul that, though he wrote well, he had a weak personality and was a poor preacher. "When he gets here you will see that there is nothing great about him, and you have never heard a worse preacher." That struck a raw nerve, but Paul's response is not an overreaction: "If I am a poor speaker," he wrote, "at least I know what I am talking about" (2 Corinthians 10:10; 11:6, *The*

Living Bible). He then goes on patiently instructing and encouraging them and assuring them of his continuing love and concern.

The overly sensitive individual is often hypercritical. He tends to project his own self-rejection onto others in the form of either criticism, sarcasm, or some other thinly veiled form of hostility. A woman who had made amazing spiritual growth in a Yokefellow group wrote me as follows:

> I hadn't been getting along well with people. They irritated and angered me, and made me resentful; yet from somewhere inside of me I felt a great loneliness that would rise up and consume me. I did not know what to do at these times except to strike out at those around me in the hope that they would notice me, even though I knew I was most obnoxious.
>
> When I entered my Yokefellow group over two years ago I was driven by a fear that overwhelmed me — a fear that some day I might kill another person. . . . I hated everyone around me, and most of all myself, for the person I had become. I fluctuated between suicidal depression and violence aimed at others. The Yokefellow group first showed me that there was a way to handle the violence within me, by facing each resentment as it came, dealing with it, and releasing it. I learned that if I hoarded these resentments, sooner or later there would be an explosion over which I had no control — something like an atom bomb. What a relief now that I have learned to handle my anger!
>
> I am particularly grateful to Yokefellows and the weekly evaluation slips[2] for putting into words the feelings I have always known I had, but couldn't verbalize. I had knowledge of my feelings before joining the group, but not the insight to go along with the emotions. I was living on pure emotion, and was headed for my third breakdown, and knew I must try, with God's help to put a stopper in the basin before I went down the drain for the last time.

5. *Self-accepting people learn to handle their anger appropriately.*

Many people firmly believe that all anger is evil. This attitude usually originates in a false religious teaching that assumes that to be "truly Christian" one must avoid displaying anger at all costs. However, I have found some persons who, though not reared in a religious environment, learned from parents or other authority figures that all anger is forbidden.

Albert, a young man in his late twenties, discussed with me

the problem of his uncontrollable anger. In the army he had at various times been demoted, censured, and almost courtmartialed for his violent displays of anger toward superior officers. I said, "Albert, you are assuming that anger is the problem, and I think it is only the symptom. The problem is probably fear, so deeply buried that you are unaware of it. It manifests itself as anger. Let's search for the ancient fear."

"No," he said, "I know myself; it's anger. I've always had trouble with it, even as a child. Won't you pray with me that it will go away?" I replied that I would pray for a solution for whatever it was that troubled him.

Albert got no relief. A few years later, having married, he came to see me about a very disabling phobia that was causing him considerable grief. He was suffering from agoraphobia, "fear of open places." He could travel only in a very restricted area and could venture outside the limits of his self-imposed prison only if he were accompanied by his wife or some trusted friend.

I said, "Albert, we are dealing now with something that bears a relationship to your anger. Much anger originates in buried fear; and your fear that has now become a phobia with deeply buried origins can be uncovered only with intensive therapy. We have delayed too long already. Let's get to work on the buried roots of your fear. Often there is buried guilt, real or false, at the bottom. Shall we start to work?"

"No," he replied, "I don't want all this psychological stuff; I just want the simple gospel. It must be removed by prayer. Prayer can remove mountains. I am a firm believer in the Word." I said, "My friend, we will be praying only about the symptom of something much deeper, believe me." He refused to consider the possibility.

That was years ago. I saw him recently, now a man of sixty who looked seventy, shuffling along the street with a fixed, false smile that never left his face. I learned that his wife had divorced him, rather than live with his proliferation of phobias. "But," he said, with his plastic, fixed smile, "I couldn't be happier. The Lord is with me. Things are really wonderful, beautiful." He shuffled on, within the limits of his greatly constricted prison, which now includes only a few blocks, beyond which he dare not venture. Because of his refusal to search for the roots of his anger and guilt he is forever imprisoned by his fears. Nothing now can release him except death, which I believe he would welcome with his frozen smile.

ANGER AND THE BIBLE

The Bible does not condemn anger. On the contrary we read, "Be ye angry, and sin not" (Ephesians 4:26, KJV).

Jesus grew angry with the Pharisees, and a lengthy passage is devoted to his bitter denunciation of them (Matthew 23:13-39). The twelve apostles knew anger, and it erupted on occasion (Matthew 20:20-24). Paul and Barnabas had a "sharp argument" (Acts 15:36-39, TEV). At Antioch Paul and Peter (Cephas) had a determined showdown over an important theological matter (Galatians 2:11), which affected the entire church.

As indicated in chapter 1, there are three main ways anger can be handled:

1. We can *express* it, which may or may not be appropriate, depending on the circumstances. We learn by trial and error and example when and how anger can be used creatively.

2. It may be *suppressed*, meaning that we are aware of the anger, but choose for whatever reason to avoid an angry confrontation. It may not be appropriate.

3. Anger may be *repressed*, which means to deny that we are angry. This is called "inwardly directed hostility," for instead of becoming aware of the anger and dealing with it, the super ego (roughly, conscience) tells us that "all anger is bad," and an instantaneous mechanism assures us that we are not angry at all.

This would seem like a good response to anger, were it not for the fact that repressing (denying) an emotion as powerful as anger can do enormous harm to a person. There is a lengthy list of physical and emotional symptoms that can result from lying to ourselves about our anger.

A Yokefellow group member wrote about her buried anger:

> The spiritual growth evaluation slips which I received really pinpointed my problem. I had been aware of fear, but the slips enabled me to find my buried anger. I was not aware of all the anger I had in me. And, along with this, my self-concept has improved tremendously. For the first time in my life I feel important — really important, just because I am me. I have learned to be honest with myself and with God. I've learned to accept myself, and the most beautiful discovery of all is that

God *accepts me as I am!* When you know this, you can accept yourself. . . . The group experience was wonderful. What beautiful people! I experienced real love — love for me as I am, and also for what I could become. I definitely plan to be in another group. . . .

A NICE PLACE TO VISIT

6. *Self-accepting people do not live in the past.*

A friend described a visit he and his wife made to their old hometown. On their return his wife said, "The past is a nice place to visit, but I wouldn't want to live there." People who live in the past, or devote a vast amount of time to reminiscing about their past, have very little self-acceptance. They feel that they have very little value apart from what happened to them "way back when."

As a child I lived for a time in a tiny Texas town. It had no paved streets, and only one block, on one side, had a sidewalk. The arrival of the evening train was the big event of the day. I often stood and watched those sophisticated people sitting up there in the dining car looking down on me. Some voice within me said, "Some day *I'll* sit in one of those dining cars with the rest of the rich people, and I'll travel through this town and look down on all the people on the station platform." It was a childish ambition, but it was real.

Years later I did ride the train through that little Texas town. I sat in the dining car and looked out over the station platform. It was terrible! There was not a soul in sight. A scrawny chicken scratched for something in the dust. The past is not even a good place to visit, sometimes.

A physiological process takes place that tends to make many older people dwell on the past. Insufficient oxygen reaches the brain, memory for recent events fades, but happenings of long ago are remembered with great fidelity. Such people, if they are talkative and have nothing to keep their minds busy, can become a dreadful bore to younger persons. The ancient past is not all that interesting to others. It can be an act of kindness to listen for a time to the infinite details of long ago, but even the most loving and patient listener grows weary. Older persons would do well to live in the present, and forego the one-sided pleasure of dredging up minutiae from the distant past.

7. *Self-accepting people do not expect others to make them happy, or meet all their needs.*

A woman who consulted me about a marriage problem seemed to be making unreasonable demands of her husband Some of her expectations were reasonable, but the rest, I felt, were leftover needs from childhood. I said, "I expect your husband is capable of meeting most of your valid needs, but many of your expectations seem to be childhood needs your parents failed to meet. If you continue demanding that your husband meet both your childhood and adult needs, you will drive him right out of the nest."

"But he *ought* to meet my needs," she said. "I have a right to expect it! What is marriage for? He's selfish not to meet these needs. If he really loved me. . . ." She went on for a long time, in a strained, petulant, demanding voice. I was saddened that her parents had not given her the love she required, for it had left her an unfulfilled, complaining woman, making unrealistic demands.

When I explained that no one person can meet all of our needs, she looked at me blankly. "But that shouldn't be! It isn't right. Why does anyone get married then?" Her marriage ended in divorce, and she is still fruitlessly searching for a man who will meet *all* of her needs.

No One Can *Make* You Happy

No one can make us happy. Others may contribute to our happiness, but it is childish and unrealistic to expect someone else to *make* us happy. Sigmund Freud wrote, "What is called happiness in its narrowest sense comes from the satisfaction — most often instantaneous — of pent-up needs which have reached great intensity, and by its very nature can only be a transitory experience."[3]

No one is happy all the time. We must settle for that first cousin of happiness, contentment; the wise are "content with contentment," studded with occasional peaks of happiness.

In the New Testament there is a word that is translated alternately "happy" or "blessed." Most of us would settle for either one.

Jesus, having set before his disciples a whole panorama of divine principles, said, "Now you know this truth; how happy you will be if you put it into practice!" (John 13:17, TEV). Thus, whatever lasting contentment or happiness you achieve will come, not as the result of meeting "the right person" who will forever make you happy; or finding the right job, or achieving some ambition, but because you have discovered and applied some eternal principles: "Open my eyes to see wonderful things in your Word. I am but a pilgrim here on earth: how I need a map — and your commands are my chart and guide. I long for your instructions more than I can tell. . . . Those who love your laws have great peace of heart and mind and do not stumble" (Psalm 119:18-20, 165, *The Living Bible*).

Notes

[1]Alistair Cooke, *Alistair Cooke's America* (New York: Alfred Knopf Publishers, 1973).

[2]The spiritual growth evaluation slips are sent to group members in response to a "Spiritual Growth Inventory" that the members take early in the process. These inventories are available from Yokefellows, Inc., 19 Park Road, Burlingame, CA 94010.

[3]Sigmund Freud, *Dictionary of Psychoanalysis* (New York: Fawcett Publications, n.d.), with preface by Theodore Reik.

6 Self-Love Is Better for You in Every Way

6 Self-Love Is Better for You in Every Way

> Of all our infirmities, the most savage is to despise our being.
>
> — *Montaigne*

People who love themselves properly tend to have fewer illnesses, live longer, are happier, less accident-prone, and more successful, have better families and fewer troubles, and make better decisions.

That is a very broad, all-inclusive generalization. It reads at first glance like a testimonial for a patent medicine. Let's see whether there is any factual evidence to support it.

First, let it be said that there appear to be some exceptions to all rules, including this one. Bad things happen to good people, as Job discovered. Jesus died on a cross; the apostle Paul suffered innumerable hardships and indignities, including imprisonment, shipwreck, and persecution.

However, mounting scientific evidence is being amassed at a prodigious rate indicating that self-hate can play a part in everything from head colds and accident-proneness, to headaches, intestinal problems, and cancer. Let's take a look at some of the concrete scientific evidence linking disturbed emotions and illness.

EMOTIONS AND DIS-EASE

Disease originally meant, not illness, but lack of ease: dis-ease. In other words, not to be at ease within oneself promotes disease. With the discovery that illness is caused by germs, it was assumed that all one had to do in order to remain well was to avoid germs. This, however, did not explain why a person becomes ill at one time and not another; why, in the midst of a flu epidemic one could remain well, yet fall victim to the flu six months or five years later when no one else around him suffered. Why, during a cold epidemic, do some people remain seemingly immune?

Recent studies reveal that the life expectancy of American men increased by only three years between 1900 to 1970, despite all of the advances in surgery, antibiotics, anaesthesia, and the elimination of smallpox and yellow fever. Women's life expectancy increased by seven years during the same period. There appears to be some unknown factor at work, increasing longevity for women faster than for men.

Groups of researchers have been studying the relationship between emotions and illness and longevity since the late 1930s. Dr. Harold G. Wolff, a neurologist at the Cornell University Medical College and New York Hospital, was one of the pioneers in the study of psychosomatic medicine. He and his associates discovered evidence that certain life events tend to trigger many kinds of illnesses, including colds, skin disease, and tuberculosis.

Another group of researchers working along the same lines explored the relationship of emotions and illness among 5,000 patients. Life-changing events, even minor ones, such as the visit of a mother-in-law, and stress of almost any kind predisposed the patients to many different forms of illness.

They found that illness tended to follow a cluster of events that required some type of life adjustment. The changes in life pattern tended to occur in a two-week period before the onset of some illnesses, which included tuberculosis, heart disease, skin disease, hernia, and kindred ailments. Life-changing events listed were such ordinary occurrences as trouble with in-laws, a son or daughter leaving home, financial difficulties, loss of a job, changing to a different type of work, and change of residence or change in school. Even vacation, retirement, and sometimes significant personal achievement seemed related to illness. Some people are unable to accept outstanding good news. It is out of harmony with their self-image and hence causes emotional stress, the forerunner of illness in many instances.

Ten different life changes were assigned a value, the one rated at 100 being death of a spouse, with these following: divorce, marital separation, jail term, death of a close family member, personal injury, marriage, being fired, marital reconciliation, retirement.

One group of researchers worked with 2,500 officers and enlisted men aboard three U.S. Navy cruisers. They gathered life-change data for six months preceding embarkation, and health change data for a six-month period starting with the beginning of the cruise. Results showed that the men in the high-risk group (those having the greatest number of life changes) suffered nearly ninety percent more illnesses than the low-risk group.

Stress, Emotions, and Self-Esteem

On the basis of weighty evidence, scientists now believe that beyond all possibility of doubt there is a close relationship between *stress* — from whatever source — and illness.

Medical men at the famous Oschner Clinic of New Orleans believe that seventy-six percent of the people who visit the clinic are suffering from psychosomatic illnesses, rather than diseases of physical origin. The disturbance is real, of course, but it has an emotional component. The school system of one of the largest cities in California estimated that seventy-five percent of ailments reported by children are emotionally induced.

Let's take a look at accidents. A considerable body of evidence indicates that, as Carl Jung postulated, the less well integrated a person is, the more adverse circumstances he seems to attract to himself. During forty-six years of counseling I have had ample opportunity to observe thousands of people and their reactions to life. I recall many persons who seemed to attract accidents, illness, and disaster as a magnet attracts iron filings. These were invariably either insecure, fearful, apprehensive individuals, who, though often outwardly cheerful, inwardly were self-rejecting persons, or individuals experiencing severe inner conflicts. Some attracted frequent illnesses, others were given to frequent hospital stays, while many were repeatedly involved in accidents.

As Jung has pointed out, the better integrated an individual is; that is, the more self-esteem he possesses, the more "good things" he attracts to himself. Jung did not explain how it worked; he simply made the observation.

Conflict, Self-Hate, and Failure

I recall a young minister whom I had occasion to know quite well over a period of fifteen years. He had ability and drive, despite a fairly limited educational background. During the period I knew him he was hospitalized a number of times with severe and inexplicable infections of a very virulent type — always the same kind. These hospitalizations invariably followed periods of severe stress in his church.

He suffered a number of accidents for which he did not seem to be directly responsible. Finally I noticed a gradual change. He became rather manic — excited, tense, and very "high." His friends interpreted it as a strong dose of enthusiasm, for he was embarking on a large expansion program. I learned later that about this time he began to drink excessively.

Eventually he ended up with a series of hospitalizations, followed by a stay in a mental hospital. Upon release, there was more heavy drinking. He finally disintegrated completely. He sought no form of counseling from any source and avoided me during his period of great stress. He ultimately disappeared from the scene after writing a number of bad checks. His was a complete emotional, spiritual, physical, and moral disintegration, which was tragic to watch.

It would be easy to judge him as simply a moral failure. My conviction is that his deep-seated sense of inferiority made it difficult for him to accept himself as a person of worth. He attempted to compensate for his inferiority complex by attaining some significant goals. When that effort failed, and he tried to deaden his disappointment with alcohol, he lost all hope. It is possible, too, that some metabolic dysfunction was at work, either causing or caused by his various personal disasters.

Joseph was a slave in Egypt, though a very valued and trusted one. When his employer's wife sought to seduce him, he might have rationalized it this way: "If I do not give in to her demands, she will get me into trouble. Survival is important. I don't want this scheming woman to become my enemy." And besides, there was his own ever-present sex drive to underscore such a rationalization.

You know the story. He rejected her advances. Then as now, "hell hath no fury like a woman scorned." She raised a cry, claiming that he had tried to attack her. Joseph ended up in jail (Genesis 39).

Prison is a lonely place, and prison fare has never been very good. In ancient Egypt it must have been rotten. We are not told how long Joseph languished in his cell, but surely it was an unpleasant reminder that the path of virtue can be rough.

Everyone likes a happy ending. But let's leave him in prison for the time being. Prison life is hard, but Joseph knows one thing: he is innocent and can sleep with a clear conscience! He has his self-respect. He can love himself properly. He has done nothing wrong. If he rots in prison, as millions have done throughout history, he can live with himself through the cold nights and the lonely days. Whether the story ends happily or otherwise is not the point, because virtue does not always get one out of prison, or bring wealth and fame. The honest, decent, moral person in some instances will suffer injustice, with only the comforting assurance that he does not deserve it. In his despair he can live with himself, and love himself for doing right. It's hard to do the will of God, but it's hell if you don't.

Patients Need Love and Reassurance

The vast majority of patients whom a physician sees in the course of any given day are there because they do not love themselves properly. Many have a physical ailment, it is true, but, as one outstanding medical man told me, "Ninety-eight percent of the people who come to me would get well if they never saw a physician. They need reassurance, which is another name for love. Medication, pills, prescriptions, tests, and the loving concern that I and my staff give them are symbols of the love they need. And I do not deprecate their need and our response in the slightest."

One physician states that "pills are often substitutes for the time and personal attention the doctor cannot give. The more pills patients can get from their physician, the more they feel he cares for them. Refusing them medication really upsets them. They think we are withholding precious help out of lack of sympathy."

Another medical man stated that patients often seek hospitalization because in that way they can be certain of a daily visit from their physician and sympathy and attention from their family and friends.

Dr. Robert Baumler, writing in *Physician's Management Journal*, says, "Some hospital patients repeatedly flash the nursing desk to adjust a pillow, or a door opening, or curtains, as a way of making the nurse indicate 'I love you.' If a daughter can get a doctor out to see her old mother, particularly if he can be summoned immediately and somewhat imperiously, the parent will have to think the daughter loves her very much."

Let's face it: There are many millions of lonely people in the world. Some of them are surrounded by family and friends but are still lonely. It is a primal need for love that was never filled in childhood. The event is in the past; the emotion is in the person, in the present. That is, the deprivation of love may have occurred in childhood thirty or fifty years ago, but the *feeling* — "I am not loved" — still resides in the individual. Such a person may go through life unaware of the unfulfilled need for love, conscious only of recurring illness, accidents, or of the fact that life is not working right. The message is: Love me, care for me, visit me, listen to me, meet my needs.

These people, of course, have little or no self-love. They do not consciously manipulate. They are not aware that they are being devious and troublesome. The child encapsulated within the adult is still sending the same message that began in the crib: "Notice me, listen to me, come touch me, hold me, cuddle me — let me know I am loved. I need you." Time does not diminish the ancient need. If anything, time intensifies it. And as normal defenses and fulfillment diminish, the original need is felt more keenly. This is one reason older people sometimes become demanding and childish and unreasonable. They have come full circle. An aging person who received adequate love as a child, or who learned later the art of self-love, seldom becomes a crochety, irrascible nuisance. Old age does not do anything for you except to make you *more* of what you are. What one was at thirty or fifty is simply intensified at seventy or ninety.

Emotions and Cancer

Writers in a medical journal report a twenty-year study in Europe involving 3,200 cancer patients. They concluded that "malignancies are preceded by major and unresolved emotional stresses." High-cancer-risk persons, they said, tended to experience the following:

1. A breakdown in interpersonal relationships early in life, resulting in a sense of isolation and a corresponding sense of uncertainty in relationships with others.

2. The patient was unable to recognize fully, or express, feelings of aggression and anger.

3. There was a tendency to ignore and repress inner emotional conflicts.

4. Frequently the patient had experienced the loss of some-

one close to him and sometimes blamed himself consciously or otherwise for the loss. This was usually followed by depression and a subsequent mood of despair and hopelessness. This does not mean that people who have any of these tendencies are likely to get cancer or that the psychological causes mentioned here are solely responsible for disease. There are other factors, such as predisposition toward cancer.

Some scientists speculate that, while it is quite possible that cancer of various kinds may be caused by a virus, some emotional states will cause a person to become a better host for one of the cancer viruses. The person who loves, respects, and accepts himself is not so easily disturbed as others. He is not so subject to stress, disease, or disaster.

One who loves God, himself, and others is fulfilling the whole law of God (Matthew 5:43-48). This is not merely a law which Jesus picked out of the Old Testament, brushed off, and offered anew as an arbitrary religious requirement for people to live up to. Rather, Jesus was restating and reaffirming a timeless principle of life. It is basic, so fundamental that we disobey or ignore it to our own destruction. One who obeys this basic principle by loving God, others, and himself, is fulfilling all of the other laws (Galatians 5:14).

SELF-ESTEEM AND DEPRESSION

Let's take the matter of depression. There is the periodic or cyclical type of depression. Most people experience this to some degree from time to time, either as the result of accumulated stress or some disappointment or combination of factors.

Then there is the deep, all-encompassing type of depression that is almost beyond description. Life seems hopeless and useless. Death often seems preferable. Many people who attempt suicide are in the depths of this type of depression. There is a sense in which they are not "sane"; that is, they are not in full possession of all their faculties. The entire organism — physical, emotional, and spiritual — has been overloaded.

When a person is seriously depressed over an extended period of time, there is often some degree of malnutrition. The diet may be adequate by normal standards, but in depressed states it is not just the mind that is undergoing depression; the entire system — mental, physical, and emotional — is "down," functioning under par. Under severe emotional stress or depression the body does not absorb vitamins and minerals as efficiently as under normal conditions.

Nothing can be more devastating to a person in deep depression than to be told to "snap out of it," "look on the bright side of things," "count your blessings," "think how much worse off many people are." Another futile approach is to urge a depressed person to "have faith."

I recall a woman who, after her second cancer operation, went into deep depression. Her well-meaning friends urged numerous cheery books upon her, offered vast amounts of advice, and sought to show her how to pray more effectively. Two of them assured her, as Job's "comforters" did, that there must be some serious malfunction in her spiritual life. All were certain that if only she prayed hard enough, she could overcome the horrible depression that descended over her and enveloped her like a black cloud.

In a number of counseling sessions I could discover no apparent reason for her depression, other than her deeply buried fear of death, intensified by her guilt-inducing friends. I sent her to a psychiatrist friend, and told him that there was no apparent reason for her depression other than fear, and guilt over not being able to resolve the problem with prayer. After some experimentation, he found a combination of antidepressants and tranquilizers that met her needs. This was, as I told her, not a solution for the problem, but would handle the symptom. She rapidly regained her normally cheerful attitude, and we began to work on the problem of her false guilt and the understandable fear that had precipitated the crisis. In her depressed state no form of talk therapy could reach her; but, relieved of the symptoms, she responded rapidly and in a relatively short time was able to dispense with the medication.

HEART ATTACKS, EMOTIONS, AND SELF-ESTEEM

It is now recognized that there is usually an emotional component in high blood pressure. This is also true in heart attacks. Drs. Friedman and Rosenman of San Francisco point out the factors that can contribute to a heart attack.[1] If you tend to hurry someone with his speech by finishing his sentences for him; if you consistently do more than one thing at a time; if you are working on some problem while someone is talking to you; dictate letters to a secretary or a dictating machine while driving; or feel guilty if you are idle for a few days, or even for a few hours, you are Type

A, and are a good prospect for a heart attack. Type-B personalities, they claim, are less tense, more accepting, with a higher degree of tolerance for frustration.

Type-A personalities, they found, have an instantly aggressive response to trivial slights and threats. This in turn sets off a chain reaction of hormonal changes that can seriously impair the metabolism, with resultant build-up of fats or cholesterol in the coronary arteries.

Some Type-A people may never have a heart attack, but their temperament may make them subject to other types of physical and/or emotional disasters. Type-A individuals are quick on the trigger, impatient, low in tolerance for frustration. Why? Because they have not come to terms with life! Loving God, man, and oneself sufficiently gives one a different outlook on life. With enough of this kind of three-way love, one's entire personality changes. One develops a higher tolerance for frustration. He not only accepts himself better, he can also accept others more readily, with all of their deficiencies. He is less bothered by irritants of all kinds — noise, delay, disappointment, threatening situations, fear of the future, death, or disaster.

You have seen people who "fight traffic." They cut in and out, jam on their brakes, push ahead, tense and anxious, irritated by other drivers, and end up at their destination often angry and half-exhausted. Other drivers who may arrive thirty seconds to a few minutes later have been relaxed, flowing with traffic instead of fighting it. Traffic fighters usually are Type-A persons, who fight life, the clock, and members of the family.

I am well aware of the fact that I manifest a few aspects of Type-A behavior, as does one of the authors of the book referred to. (He has had a heart attack, and has modified his behavior considerably.) I am not "wired" for a quiet, reflective, meditative life. So, by an act of will, working against a genetic and environmental tendency toward constant activity, I take myself by the back of the neck during the day and get myself into a reclining chair. I first turn off my telephone and close the door. This indicates that I am not available to anyone, for any purpose. Fighting down the ancient "parent" tape that urges me to "keep busy, don't just sit there, run and get me the hammer," I put on the headphones and turn on the stereo. I listen to some quieting music, sometimes to a meditation tape. Occasionally I become so relaxed that I go to sleep for a few minutes.

Jesus seems to have alternated between periods of intense

activity, and quiet receptivity. There was the time he gave orders to go to the other side of the lake when a crowd approached, for he was physically exhausted (Matthew 8:18). On another occasion he took the disciples to the coast, quite some distance away, for a period of quiet rest (Matthew 15:21).

He frequently arose "a great while before day" for prayer and meditation (Mark 1:35). Only by taking such periods of rest and meditation was he able to remain calm amidst the confusion caused when the crowds pressed in upon him.

We know in our heads that a daily quiet time leads to greater serenity. No one denies it. We recognize our need for meditation and prayer — to be alone and pull the tattered edges of our souls together. If this be so, then what perverse streak is it within us that causes us to fill every day to the brim and cram each hour to overflowing with tasks that, if left undone, would not cause cosmic disaster?

I suggest that the answer is simple: We do not love ourselves. Because we don't, we gain some satisfaction and false self-esteem from working until we are gray-faced with fatigue, complaining the while about our busy schedules. At its core, it is substituting busy-ness for creativity and serenity.

ARE YOU *DRIVEN*, OR DRIVING?

"He restoreth my soul" was never said by anyone in a frantic race against time, panting and out of breath, guilt-ridden over not getting more done. I confess to feeling more virtuous when I have accomplished a great deal in a given day. I shall never completely erase my "parent tape." But I am muting it. As I write this, I have taken off two weeks — by an act of the will, because my schedule was very full — to go and sit in a beautiful spot near Carmel, California, overlooking the Pacific. I can write, read, think, walk on the beach, photograph flowers, watch the breakers, write some more, prowl around Carmel, relax, read a mystery story, and still get in five to seven hours of writing a day.

It is a happy compromise I have made with my "driven self," the one that responds to the "parent tape" urging me to get in motion and not rest for a minute. I am fighting a moderately successful battle against what, for some strange reason, is called the Protestant Work Ethic. (I don't know many Buddhists who are compulsive workers, but I imagine numerous Catholics and any number of Jews as well as atheists are addicted.)

By way of emphasis, let's go over some of these important factors again:

1. People who practice the three-way love principle tend to have fewer physical and emotional problems. There is ample scientific evidence to validate this. More important, Jesus stressed this as the *supreme principle,* so it must have tremendous importance. Obeying this universal law is not something we do to make God happy. He's getting along fine. It is for our own well-being that we obey this injunction.

2. Those who experience this three-way love are less accident-prone. This has been observed by such psychiatrists as C. G. Jung and has been validated in human experience by many observers. "Those who love your laws have great peace of heart and mind," reads one of the Psalms (119:165, *The Living Bible*). When we love these cosmic principles instead of thinking of them as burdensome religious observances, we are eligible for the peace and serenity of which the psalmist speaks.

3. A proper self-love can help prevent heart attacks and illness. This is being validated by medical men in research conducted over a period of forty-five years. The organism was meant to function better when there is an absence of excessive stress. All of the organs undergo tension for which they were not designed when we drive ourselves too long and too hard.

4. We become more likable, more acceptable persons when we acquire self-esteem. Loving ourselves, we are less touchy, less prone to be judgmental, and more capable of deeper friendships. People may not know precisely what is wrong with us when we are filled with self-hate or a weak self-image, but they know *something* is wrong. They tend to relate to us more freely and openly when we like ourselves better.

5. The self-accepting person is far less likely to suffer depression. In a deep depression, there is usually some form of self-hate originating in a sense of loss, failure (or fear of failure), guilt, or some serious threat to the individual. One who practices the three-way love principle consistently has inner resources on which he can draw in a crisis.

6. Those with a positive regard for themselves tend to *flow with* life, instead of *fighting* it. They feel more in harmony with the universe, less out of synchronization. Life becomes less of a struggling, crushing, competitive game where someone always loses and some may get hurt, and more of a pleasurable experience. In short, self-love is better for you in every way.

In another chapter we consider the day-to-day specific steps by which you can acquire a greater degree of self-esteem.

Notes

[1]Meyer Friedman, M.D., and Ray Rosenman, M.D., *Type A Behavior and Your Heart* (New York: Fawcett Publications, 1975).

7 Steps in Learning to Love Yourself, I

7 Steps in Learning to Love Yourself, I

> Though there certainly exists an explicit teaching of the gospel in the church, there also exists an implicit . . . fostering of low self-image as a desirable goal for Christian people. As long as people are encouraged to think more lowly of themselves than they ought, breakdown will continue to be very real.[1]

There is a quaint little story about a very small frog that fell into a deep rut. Try as he would, he couldn't jump out. Some frog friends came by and looked in. "What's the matter?" they asked. "I can't get out; I've tried all morning," he replied.

They couldn't help him, so they went their way. That afternoon they happened to pass the spot again and looked in. Their little friend was gone. Searching about, they found him hopping around in the grass. "We thought you couldn't get out." "I couldn't," he said, "but a big truck came along and I *had* to." A crisis, a threat, or pain can be a powerful motivator.

There is something within most of us that would like to believe in Santa Claus, magic, and simplistic answers. It is this relic of childhood that leads a woman to feel that all her problems will be resolved if she can just meet the right man; or if her husband will stop drinking, or stay home more, or do more of this and less of that.

The residual childhood belief in magic leads some men to believe in get-rich-quick schemes, or that a shaky marriage will automatically improve without effort. The disillusioning truth is that in this life we have to work for what we get. Most people have to work for a living. Good marriages don't just happen. They have to be worked out. Good things seldom "fall" into our lives. Growth requires effort.

Many people make an effort to resolve the problem of low self-esteem, but do it in the wrong way. Because it is largely unconscious, they are not aware that it is often a destructive course of action.

"So intensely does a man feel the need of a positive view of himself, that he may evade, repress, distort his judgment, disintegrate his mind, in order to avoid coming face-to-face with the facts that would affect his self-appraisal adversely. A man who has chosen or accepted irrational standards by which to judge himself, can be driven all his life to pursue flagrantly self-destructive goals — in order to assure himself that he possesses a self-esteem which in fact he does not have."[2]

An individual is driven to seek false self-esteem because it appears to be the only alternative to facing life with his inadequacies, much as an alcoholic feels compelled to drink by the vague but powerful feeling that without another drink he is helpless and incompetent. Both the alcoholic (and one might add drug addict, "workaholic," and compulsive eater) and the one attempting to fake self-esteem are doomed to failure. There is always the day of reckoning, the unveiling of the cringing, powerless, self-rejecting person now devoid of his false defenses.

There is a vast difference between faking and consciously embarking on a positive course of action aimed at building genuine self-esteem. One may feel hypocritical and vaguely uneasy when beginning a course of action to build up a proper self-love; but one feels phony only because the new pattern of behavior is unfamiliar and seems awkward at first.

Some realistic steps you can take to help you achieve a better self-image are given below. Merely reading them will probably do you very little good. You will need to pick out one specific step at a time, write it on a card, and carry it with you. Refer to it often during the week. Jot down on the card ways in which you can implement your goal. Carrying the card with you and looking at it frequently will activate your unconscious mind. Remember, as you begin, that there are no free lunches, no magic cures, no simple solutions for lifelong problems. It took you all those years to become the person you are. It will take time to change your self-image.

I am not suggesting a palpitating, frenzied struggle, but a

single-minded long-range program. The Bible stresses the importance of this singleness of purpose. "You will seek me and find me; when you seek me with all your heart" (Jeremiah 29:13, RSV). Eric Fromm suggests that learning to love requires giving it priority. In the acquiring of an art, disciplined effort is essential, whether it is learning to play a guitar, to paint, or rear children; and diligent, disciplined effort is most often achieved alone. One may learn principles in a class, a church service, or a group, but one usually achieves competence in any art or skill by practicing it alone.

Here are some of the means by which one achieves a proper self-love:

Accept emotionally, as well as intellectually, the idea that a proper self-love is all right, and that God expects it. Jesus commanded it when he taught that the supreme law is to love God with all of your heart, mind, soul, and strength and to love your fellow-man *as you love yourself.* Loving yourself properly is not egotism. Egotistical people actually dislike themselves intensely. Only those who accept and like themselves are capable of true humility. Such persons tend to view themselves with amused friendly tolerance. They are not engaged in a frantic, breathless campaign to win approval or praise. Since they accept themselves, they do not need the recognition of others to bolster their sense of identity.

Give up self-condemnation. Criticizing or condemning yourself generates more self-hate. It is just as wrong to keep up a constant barrage of self-criticism as it is to be critical of others; it is terribly destructive.

MOST SELF-HATE HAS ROOTS IN CHILDHOOD

One morning my wife served me coffee in bed. (To avoid charges of male chauvinism I hasten to add that I sometimes do the same for her.) In a careless gesture I upset the coffee over a bedside table, half a dozen books, the bed, and the rug. I had done the same thing once before. I exploded: "I *hate* myself when I do that!" With my wife's help I mopped up the spilled coffee, dried off the books and papers, sponged off the rug, and leaned back to think about it. It was a minor event, but I suspected that there were some major emotions involved. Why should I hate myself for an occasional bit of clumsiness? As I let my mind roam back into the distant past, I could see a little boy at the dinner table, with a youngish mother, two older sisters, and father. I saw the child grasp a big glass of milk, lose control of it, and spill the contents all over the table. I could hear mother's "Oh, you *spilled your milk!*" (It seemed like a superfluous announcement.) I could sense the irritation and impatience with which the entire family went to work mopping up the table.

I let myself relive that little kid's feeling. It was "I'm clumsy and stupid. They hate me." So now, I thought, all the rest of my life I must beat them (parents, friends, family, whoever) to the punch, and before they can judge me as awkward or stupid, I must say it myself.

I smiled as I ran that film past my inner eye. So that was the source of the statement surprised out of me, "I hate myself when I do that." It took only a few seconds to review that film, and another second or two to resolve never to say again, "I hate myself."

There had been a quick one-second flash, too, as the coffee spilled: "She (wife/mother) will be upset." But I realized instantly that my wife had never expressed the slightest irritation over minor accidents. After all, she is human and spills things too. So it was mother, really, not my wife.

A small illustration, that; but whether it be spilled coffee, or milk, or a moral lapse, one must learn to abandon self-hate. Review the incident and see how it can be avoided in the future. At that point all remorse or guilt should subside.

SHARING HELPS BUILD SELF-ESTEEM

Join a sharing group. I am not referring to Bible study or prayer groups, good as these may be under proper leadership. I am recommending a group where honesty is encouraged, without attack; where advice is considered an insult; where others listen as you share your deepest needs or hurts or longings. In short, I am thinking of the kind of group where you are accepted *as you are.* Acceptance is an important aspect of love.

Since 1957, Yokefellows, Inc.,[3] has provided material and guidance for such groups in churches of some thirty denominations. Over seventy thousand people have participated in such groups and have utilized the spiritual growth inventories[4] that enable the group members to discover their barriers to emotional and spiritual growth.

As stressed in an earlier chapter, we tend to discover our true identity in the act of self-disclosure. It helps for others to mirror what they see in us, without judgment; and normally what they see is not the marred image we project on our own inner screen.

Typical of thousands of unsolicited letters is this one from a woman who writes:

> Before joining the Yokefellow group I was considering divorce. We now have a *very* happy marital relationship. I have a deeper sense of self-worth as a woman and as a parent. Formerly I prayed only in emergencies. Now reading, meditation and prayer are as essential as eating and sleeping. At first I prayed mainly for myself. Now my prayers are almost totally for others and often I just thank God for His blessings. I am a happier, much more stable, mature person.

Distinguish between neurotic fantasies and realistic goals. Gladys, a married woman in her thirties, had a very rough childhood. She saw me weekly, and sometimes oftener, as she tried desperately to maintain her hold on sanity. She had so little self-worth that her self-hate emerged in the form of rage toward her husband and her eldest daughter. Partly as the result of her emotional instability, her husband lost his position, and the resultant financial crisis created more insecurity and anxiety in her. She was diagnosed as a paranoid schizophrenic.

During this period Gladys shared many fantasies with me. She was confident that she could become a professional singer if she were only given the chance. She composed music and recorded it on tape, which she played for me. She was pathetically determined to "be somebody," to win applause and to be looked up to. Of course, I did not seek to dissuade her or to shatter her fantasies of glory. She needed them just then.

In time her paranoia diminished. The split halves of the self began to merge in a more solid fashion and her fantasies lessened. She secured a job and appeared contented with what proved to be a fairly mundane position. Her dreams of glory vanished. She no longer needed them.

Frank's ambition illustrates a more realistic drive toward a goal that he ultimately reached. His sadistic, rejecting mother married a succession of five men. "All of them were bums," Frank said. In his early teens he announced that he was going to be a football star at a great university and a millionaire by the time he was forty. His parents, of course, ridiculed his absurd boyish fantasies.

But he made his fantasy a reality! From some unexpected source he drew strength and guidance. It never crossed his mind that he would fail to reach his goal. He did become a football star at a prestigious university. I knew him during the last ten years before he hit forty, for we spent considerable time working on his marriage. At forty he had made his million. He then resigned his position as president of the firm, and began to look around for other fields of endeavor. He wanted to do more than make money and would like to be involved in helping people.

There was a vast difference between Gladys' dream of glory and Frank's long-range goals. Gladys fantasized unrealistic attainments in order to compensate for terrifying feelings of self-hate; Frank set long-term goals toward which he worked consistently over a period of twenty-five years.

Most people find it necessary to scale down some of their childhood dreams of grandeur. Infantile megalomania, the early belief in one's omnipotence, gives way to reality. Only the individual can tell, by trial and error, which is valid ambition and which is unrealistic fantasy of glory.

MOTIVES — GOOD, BAD, AND MIXED

Check your motives. A college friend of mine once told me that his ambition was to make a lot of money and do a great deal of good in the world. Forty years later he had done neither, though I expect that if he had not had mixed motives he might have achieved one or the other of his goals.

The Taoist insight is pertinent: "When the wrong man uses the right means, the right means works the wrong way." Ambition can be laudable, a proper means to an end, but *the wrong man* with ambition may end up a failure.

"The wrong man" is one whose motives are impaired. They are faulty if he is a manipulator, if he is self-centered, if he is punitive or seeks revenge, if he is dishonest in pursuing even laudable goals, if he lacks integrity, if he seeks ease without labor.

"Blessed are the pure in heart" (Matthew 5:8) is an oft-misunderstood beatitude. For some reason the word *purity* came to have the connotation of sexual morality. But purity, as Jesus used the term, has a much wider application. It implies an absence of mixed motives, to be purely oneself without pretense. Add milk to pure water and it is no longer pure; it has become adulterated.

I once had a delightful friend who, along with his many worthwhile traits and undoubted ability, was an accomplished manipulator. When he phoned or visited me it was always for a double purpose. Any joint venture with him turned out to have a concealed purpose advantageous to him. I enjoyed his friendship, but eventually his mixed motives turned me off, and I found myself regarding him with caution. No one likes to be used consistently. I doubt if he was ever aware of this aspect of his personality. It was not my role to inform him; I had deficient personality traits of my own I was working on.

Since we all have a tendency to conceal certain things from ourselves, it can be helpful to check your motives and goals with some objective person. Friends, not wanting to hurt us, may not always be totally honest. An emotionally uninvolved counselor, or a sharing group, will come closer to reflecting back to you what they see and hear.

JESUS' FORMULA FOR BUILDING SELF-ESTEEM

Do the things that will make you like yourself better. Jesus taught some universal principles that will work for Christian, Moslem, Jew, Buddhist, or atheist. A basic one is this: "Give, and it will be given to you . . ." (Luke 6:38, RSV). Give love, sympathy, help, understanding, forgiveness, money — whatever seems indicated. This "giving attitude" can involve a simple note of appreciation to a friend; giving undivided attention to someone who needs a listening ear, and without necessarily offering advice; pausing to talk to a child, a lonely person, or a frightened dropout from society.

Jesus also said, "Give to him who begs from you, and do not refuse him who would borrow from you" (Matthew 5:42, RSV) and "Lend, expecting nothing in return" (Luke 6:35, RSV). When I lend a book I hope to have it returned, usually a futile expectation. I would hesitate to estimate the number of my books now in the hands of other people. The point of Jesus' teaching is this: He who lends and receives it back again has really done little if anything (Luke 6:34). It has cost him nothing, therefore it is nothing to be proud of. Bankers lend at interest and expect the loan to be repaid. That is their business. They do not claim any particular virtue for themselves as lenders. Nor should we, according to Jesus, think of it as a virtue if we lend and receive it back again. It becomes a virtue only if it is an open-handed gesture of love and concern with no strings.

Must we then allow ourselves to be taken advantage of by freeloaders, rip-off artists, and manipulators? I think not. Within our power, we are to do whatever is *loving and helpful* for people, but we are to use our God-given intelligence in deciding to whom and when to give or lend. It must not be done to buy their love and friendship, nor to purchase virtue, assuming that were possible.

"Give to him who asks of you." My feeling is that Jesus meant it to be taken seriously, not necessarily literally. I once signed a note for a member of my church. In effect I was lending him the money, since his credit was bad. The banker phoned me an hour or two later and said, "You can go through with this if you wish, but I want to tell you that you are not helping this man. He has lived beyond his means for years. I know him. He needs to learn to live within his income." The banker taught me a lesson. What the man needed was not my name signed on a piece of paper, but my help in sorting out his tangled financial affairs. This I finally did. It had been easier to sign his note than to help him solve his real problem. I met his real need, not the one he expressed.

MEETING THE *REAL* NEED

As a pastor, I had the same problem with alcoholics, who would turn up periodically around dusk, after the petty cash was locked up and the office secretary had gone for the day. Feeling unaccountably angry and compassionate at the same time, I would invariably give them money for food and lodging. I finally sensed that I was angry because I knew that I wasn't really helping them, and sympathetic because I genuinely hated to see them go hungry.

Eventually I learned to say to them, "No, I cannot give you any money. I will drive you to the Alcoholic Rehabilitation Center, or to the Salvation Army Farm for Alcoholics, but I will not give you cash." The first man I said that to, an alcoholic named Bob, flew into a rage and called me all the names he could think of, which were considerable. I discovered later that after leaving the church he tried panhandling for an hour or two, ending up with only enough for bus fare. He went to San Francisco and turned himself into an alcoholic rehabilitation center, where he finally got dried out. He found a job and earned enough money for bus fare back to the state where he had grown up.

There are three possible responses to pleas for help. We can give people what they ask for; we can refuse to help; or we can *discover the real* need and try to meet it, within our capacity, on our own terms. This often takes much more time and skill than to grant the individual's request. But to seek out the real need is to express love, for love is not only an emotion or attitude, it is an action.

Now we come to some of the do nots. They are just as important as the positive steps:

1. *Avoid name-dropping.* This is one of the most used and abused ploys of people who are unsure of themselves. One who uses names of important people to bolster his sense of identity is broadcasting to the world that he has so little self-worth that he has to borrow the glitter and worth of others to add to his own shabby self-esteem. "As my friend Joe was telling me the other day — he's the new mayor, you know. . . ." Reflected glory and borrowed finery are one and the same. They belong to others.

2. *Avoid negativism.* Some people with a weak self-image cannot think of constructive things to say, and settle for making negative or critical comments. I recall a man who, when his church was much smaller, held a position of some importance. As the membership grew, he was no longer a significant factor. At the conclusion of a lengthy board meeting, during which he had contributed nothing, he looked up at one of the chandeliers and said petulantly, "We'll just have to call the custodian's attention to the dead flies in these light fixtures. It looks terrible. He's not on the job." It was his only comment during a three-hour session.

   Another board member with a negative attitude was noted for adding to any motion the warning: "Perhaps we should check into the legality of this matter before proceeding further." He seldom had anything else to offer. Perfectionistic, critical, petulant people are ultimately avoided.

3. *Abstain from argumentativeness.* There are obviously times when one needs to stand up for a principle, or even for a method. That is different from being fundamentally argumentative. Self-rejecting people who have a measure of aggressiveness can often sound quarrelsome and petty.

   I recall a brilliant and otherwise pleasant man of considerable ability who was gently persistent in committee and board meetings. In denominational meetings he tended to bore in, gently, tactfully, but relentlessly, until everyone was bored and disgusted. He never learned the difference between a method and a principle. He would as readily spend an hour on some trivial method as on a major principle. He eventually lost his position, his influence, and his friends. He shared with me his deep conviction that he was being persecuted by his former friends. Paranoia had set in.

The New Testament has little to say about religion, which is referred to only twice, almost incidentally. Jesus spoke primarily about life abundant, joy, love, peace, happiness, life eternal, and human relations.

It is as though he tossed down a bunch of keys before his listeners. The trial and error involved in discovering when and where to use this or that key — that is the game. And as in any game, there are hazards, challenges, difficulties. The game need not be any more grim than tennis, or golf, or chess. A grim, joyless religion must be a monumental offense to God. Certainly it was an offense to the One who expressed the hope "that my joy may be in you, and that your joy may be full." "My peace I give to you. . . ." "If you know these things, blessed are you if you do them." "I came that they might have life, and have it abundantly. . . ." "A new commandment I give to you, that you love one another . . . " (John 15:11; 14:27; 13:17; 10:10; 13:34, RSV).

One could follow a man like that anywhere! And if we fail, it is wonderful to know that he does not condemn, but that he says to us as he did to another, "Neither do I condemn you . . . " (John 8:11).

Notes

[1]William A. Miller, *Why Do Christians Break Down?* (Minneapolis: Augsburg Publishing House, 1973).

[2]Nathaniel Branden, *The Psychology of Self-Esteem* (New York: Bantam Books, 1975).

[3]19 Park Road, Burlingame, CA 94010.

[4]The inventories involve a feedback system of bi-weekly evaluation slips for use in the groups.

8 Steps In Learning to Love Yourself, II

8 Steps In Learning to Love Yourself, II

No one knows fully what a man can achieve until,
motivated by desire, he marshalls his forces and
decides that nothing shall defeat him.

— *Germaine St. Cloud*

Before we continue with the positive steps one can take to achieve
a proper self-love, it can be profitable to look at some of the
common evasions people use:

Postponement. The road to neurosis, like the road to hell, is
paved with good intentions, long postponed. You can delay, alibi,
excuse, procrastinate, rationalize, and offer yourself a hundred
excuses, but the only way to reach any worthwhile goal is to *start*.
A great line of poetry has been turned into a cliché with a partial
truth: "They also serve who only stand and wait"; but it is truer to
state that they also *starve* who only stand and wait — starve for
the good things of life: love and friendship and self-esteem.

Alcohol. "The 'pleasure' of being drunk is obviously the
pleasure of escaping from the responsibility of consciousness.
And so are the kind of social gatherings, held for no other purpose
than the expression of hysterical chaos, where the guests wander
around in an alcoholic stupor, prattling noisily and senselessly,
and enjoying the illusion of a universe where one is not burdened
with purpose, logic, reality or awareness."[1]

In the same category are tranquilizers, both uppers and

downers. There is a legitimate place for the temporary use of tranquilizers, but they do not provide a permanent solution for the nameless dread and anxiety lodged in the subterranean chambers of the personality.

Frantic socialization. Those who cannot bear to be alone and must seek out companions in order to quiet the pathological anxiety originating in self-rejection are akin to the loners whose anxiety is intensified by social contact; both are seeking an escape from reality.

The geographical cure. This is a false solution sought by those who believe that a new job, or a new husband or wife, or a new house (clothes, car, trips, gadgets) will provide release from the ever-present anxiety being generated by low self-esteem.

Depression. Most serious depression originates in self-hate and is an unconscious effort to shut off feelings. Depression is not an emotion, but results from the shutting down of feelings, to *avoid* feeling. The defense system, sometimes our friend but often our enemy, offers an illusionary escape from whatever feelings we would have to face otherwise.

Compulsive work. The compulsive worker is running from something. Sometimes it is an effort to avoid hearing an ancient "parent tape" accusing one of being lazy. Turning out a vast amount of work, refusing to take a vacation, bringing home work from the office, finding eighteen hours of work to do and never getting it finished — all these are efforts to win temporary respite from some muted but incessant voice that says, "You're no good unless you keep busy."

Compulsive sloth. The compulsive worker can at least win temporary self-approval and passing admiration for the amount of work done, but the slothful person gets only condemnation. Whether it is the child staring dreamingly out of the school window, or the housewife slouched hour after hour before the television set (or the uncommunicative husband watching TV with a grunt, a grouch, and a can of beer), or someone who is unmotivated and simply cannot get started, such a person confuses and antagonizes those of us who were taught that the devil has work for idle hands. And if we happen to be diligent, hard-working, never-take-a-rest kind of persons, the lazy person challenges our sense of "oughtness." The truth is that the unmotivated or indolent individual is reacting to life in the only way he knows how at the moment. Accusations and admonitions worsen the situation. Intensive therapy is usually indicated.

Then there is the retreat into sickness, into excessive busyness, into bookishness, as with the professional student, and into a fantasy world, an escape from reality.

The only creative solution is to get into motion with a practical course of action. Let's look at some more of these possibilities:

Start paying compliments. It will not be easy if you are unaccustomed to offering praise. Form the habit of noticing what people are wearing. If it is something new, a simple "Say, I like that!" will suffice. No one was ever insulted by a sincere compliment. Everyone wants to be noticed. If a friend has a new car, or wins a promotion, you can either react with envy and wonder how he managed it, or say, "Congratulations on the new job," or car, or whatever.

In her widely syndicated column, Dear Abby replied to a woman who asked what kind of response one could give to a person who showed a picture of a child who was anything but attractive. Abby suggested that an appropriate response would be, "You must be very proud." Good advice. A perfectly honest reply ("What an ugly child") would be devastating to the parent; but there is a higher law than honesty. It is the principle of love. The New Testament admonition about "speaking the truth in love" (Ephesians 4:15) is sound advice.

Psychologist William James pointed out that feelings follow actions. If you do not feel comfortable or sincere when you first start paying honest compliments, "act as if" you felt sincere, and in time you will not feel phony. Even if you do feel hypocritical at first, remember that *it is never phony to act appropriately.*

Give love and understanding. You may feel lonely or depressed yourself, and it would be nice if someone visited you and expressed his love and concern. You may wait a long time. So begin at the giving point. Through your church, your lodge, or office, find the names of shut-ins who are lonely and in need of regular visits. Whatever it is that you would like for others to do for you, do that for them, is the teaching of Jesus. You will not be doing it entirely for them; you will derive important benefits too. You will like yourself better. It is a great way to build a proper self-esteem.

I once knew a desperately depressed and lonely woman who

had experienced ten years of emotional illness. Long before she had recovered sufficiently to hold down a job she sought out two elderly women, members of her church, and visited them regularly. She spent hours listening, having occasional meals with them, and driving them places. The shut-ins were worse off than she, and she decided to give them love and attention. I counseled with her during part of her lengthy recovery and observed the therapeutic benefits of her program of visitation.

In most towns and cities there are retirement and convalescent homes. Many of the people in these homes are terribly lonely. Some do not have a visitor from one month to the next. A phone call will provide the necessary information regarding visiting hours.

What if you don't really want to visit the lonely? *If you don't feel like it, do it anyway!* Remember that feelings follow actions. *You're* tired. *You* need attention; why should *you* be the one giving and loving when you need it as much as anyone else? Because it's good for you! You can wallow in your misery, or you can get into motion and feel better. The New Testament tells the story of ten lepers who approached Jesus for healing (Luke 17:12-19). He told them to go and show themselves to the priests for verification of their healing, which had not yet occurred. The account says, *"As they went, they were cleansed"* (v. 14, KJV). You may not be healed of whatever it is that troubles you until you get into motion.

Begin the practice of forgiving yourself. There are two aspects to forgiveness. One is God's forgiveness upon our confession and repentance. The other is existential forgiveness, or the cleansing that takes place when at last we are able to forgive ourselves. Most people have little difficulty believing that God forgives. The problem is in forgiving oneself.

THE PRAYER OF AFFIRMATION

The Twenty-third Psalm is a prayer of affirmation in which the psalmist affirms to his inner self what he knows intellectually about God. You can employ the same technique. Write this formula on a card and carry it with you indefinitely. Repeat it ten or a dozen times a day for three months. After you have reached your goal and are able to forgive yourself fully, the old feelings will probably return, in time. It will not take as long the second time, nor the third or the fourth. Old habit patterns such as self-condemnation tend to reassert themselves but to a lesser degree. Here is the formula:

> I am neither good nor bad, I am both.
> I am neither honest nor dishonest, I am both.
> I am neither generous nor selfish, I am both.
> (Make up your own list to fit your situation.)
> But God accepts me, forgives me, and loves me, and
> I now accept, forgive, and love myself.

I once saw a cartoon involving two insects, a little bug and a praying mantis. The tiny buy looked up at the larger insect and asked, "What kind of an insect are you?" "I'm a praying mantis," was the reply. "That's ridiculous," said the bug. "Everyone knows that insects don't pray."

In the last panel the praying mantis had the bug by the neck, squeezing hard. The little bug's eyes were bulging and rolled heavenward as he was saying frantically, "Our Father who art in heaven. . . ." The cartoonist had a powerful message, which is that with enough pain or stress, we begin to pray, to act, or do whatever seems indicated under the circumstances. Alcoholics Anonymous have as one of their axioms the basic premise that an alcoholic must "reach his bottom" before he will seek help. His "bottom" may be the loss of a job, family, savings, home, health, or all of these. At that point he gives up and calls for help. You may or may not be hurting enough to begin some of these steps. When you are, start at some point where you feel reasonably sure of success.

LEARNING TO BE QUIET

Learn to meditate. (No magic, remember? Just a lot of hard work.) Meditation can be difficult, for it involves learning to be quiet; but most people who have tried daily meditation report new feelings of peace and serenity. Try two twenty-minute periods of meditation a day, or one thirty-minute session. (Two periods are better.)

Some people say that their minds wander when they meditate. For these, Yokefellows, Inc., has produced several meditation cassettes.[2] One is titled "Meditation/Relaxation." There is a series of seven others, called *The Next Step*, which is ordered as a unit. These cassettes are helpful to many people in focusing their attention. They also provide a means of relaxation, especially helpful for those who are tense or anxious.

There is another way to meditate. Take an inspirational book and read until you find something that stimulates your thinking. *Stop right there.* Shut the book, close your eyes and ask yourself,

"What would it involve if I were to apply that principle to my life?" Roll that question over in your mind until you have exhausted the possibilities. Then read again. It is important to stop *immediately* when you find a thought or principle that applies to you. To read beyond that point is "greedy reading," stuffing the mind with intellectual concepts without taking time to meditate on them and digest them emotionally.

GET INTO MOTION

Join an activity group. Every community has such groups. I recall a young man who was having serious difficulty in his marriage, which finally ended in divorce. I found him to be terribly immature. He seemed to lack ordinary common sense and consequently· was in all manner of difficulty. He appeared to be a fairly hopeless case. After the breakup of the marriage I did not see him for two or three years.

The next time I saw him he was emerging from the weekly meeting of the Toastmaster's Club of which he had become an officer. I sensed a remarkable change in him. He was poised, relaxed, and friendly. It wasn't a put-on either; he was genuine. Since he had been learning to express himself, he had gained self-confidence. He had matured to a remarkable degree.

People need people. We are gregarious beings who do not grow well in isolation. Some people who are very shy rationalize their sedentary habits with such generalizations as "People are shallow" or "I'd much rather read a good book." The rationalizations may have an element of truth, but the fact remains that we tend to grow emotionally and spiritually "in community," working, worshiping, studying, and having fellowship with other people.

I recall two men with radically different approaches who united with the church of which I was senior minister. One was a diffident young man suffering from a serious inferiority complex. He had an outgoing, brilliant brother who had once been active as a leader among our young people. The shy brother joined and soon asked to be allowed to teach a class. He was definitely not teacher material. Sundry other opportunities were offered him, all of which he rejected. He was determined to be a teacher or nothing, and eventually drifted away.

It is readily understandable that, with his monumental inferiority complex, he felt a need for a job with some prestige. (Abraham Lincoln was once approached by a man from his home state who asked to be appointed to a very important position. Lincoln said, "That job requires a big man." The rather inadequate applicant replied, "Mr. President, appoint me to the job and I'll automatically *be* a big man.")

The other man who united with the church was a kindly physician, gentle, friendly, and unassuming. He said, "Dr. Osborne, I'm available for any job you have. Nothing is too small." The church hostess needed someone to help serve the food at the family-night dinners. He assented readily. And what a cheerful, effective disher-upper he was! He speeded up the waiting line by fifty percent over anyone else who had ever done the job. In the many years he belonged to the church he served in a dozen or more capacities. Nothing was beneath him and he proved capable in many major capacities as well.

Jesus said, when observing how the Twelve jockeyed for position and prestige: "He who is greatest among you shall be your servant" (Matthew 23:11, RSV). Humble service need not be humiliating, except to the person with a mammoth inferiority complex. At a church "clean-up" project I watched a federal judge vigorously loading junk on a truck, and a society matron scrubbing the kitchen floor.

Listening Is an Act of Love

Learn to listen. Listening is an art, and few people acquire it. A good listener is rare indeed. Listening with an abstracted air and glazed eyes is all too common. There are those who listen just long enough to find suitable opening to interject their "Yes, and that reminds me of something that happened to me. . . ."

Since listening is an act of love and of caring, it is surprising that so few people express loving concern in this way. Being a good listener is far more important than being a good talker.

I am not suggesting the self-abasing attitude that says, "I'm nobody; I don't matter; don't pay any attention to me. I'm too timid to enter into the conversation, so I'll just listen." This wallflower type of passivity is not it at all. You are entitled to enter into the conversation. But the thing to be deplored in almost any group is the fact that *so few people are actively listening.* There is a big difference between listening actively and passively. The active listener may manifest interest by asking, "Yes, and what happened then?" or by making some appropriate comment. Active listening involves three steps:

1. "What happened? Tell me about it."

2. Listen actively, encouraging the other to talk.
3. Validate the feeling, which calls for something like, "Yes, that was interesting. Your trip to Afghanistan sounds fascinating. I'd like to visit there sometime. Tell me more about it."

It isn't easy to affirm another person who has had a marvelous vacation in Tahiti, or experienced fabulous adventures in the Gobi desert, especially when envy is being felt in your every pore. But if you want to be a friend, you will want to practice active listening. It isn't easy to rejoice with a friend who has just bought a new Mercedes Benz; or who has had a fantastic promotion; or whose son has graduated *summa cum laude* from Harvard and has fabulous offers from IBM, General Motors, and Standard Oil. But it is important to develop your sense of self-worth by learning to express interest and concern *even when it is difficult*.

Almost anyone can express love to the lovable, compassion to the downtrodden, and congratulations to a consistent loser who has finally achieved some minor goal. It is difficult to congragulate someone who may not deserve his good fortune, or to listen to a bore when you would prefer to be almost any place else. It is in such circumstances as these that one builds self-esteem and acquires genuine self-love by practicing the loving art of listening.

Choose goals well within your reach. The get-to-the-top-in-a-hurry syndrome has severe limitations. You may see people in some organization who are chosen for significant positions of leadership or promotion who appear to have less ability than you. You can let it make you bitter and cynical, or you can stick it out. Your sterling qualities may not have been discovered yet.

In selecting goals, make sure that there is not too great a chance of failure. It is best to work toward goals that are readily attainable. Too many defeats can be disheartening and ultimately defeating.

And patience! (No magic, remember?) Any worthwhile achievement takes time. I once said to a group of ministers, "You have to be at least thirty, or married, to have learned that life is frustrating." A fine-looking young man in the front row said, "I'm twenty-nine, unmarried, and I'm already frustrated!" I replied, "You're to be congratulated. You're precocious."

In the selection of goals it is important to avoid some common "defense-goals," that is, goals that are unconsciously utilized in an effort to achieve self-esteem but are really a futile defense against feelings of inferiority. These illustrate the principle:

— The martyr-mother who, having no genuine identity of her own, confuses her *role* as mother with her *identity*. She has a sense of being "real" and worthwhile only as long as she can play the role of the ever-loving, always-sacrificing mother. She means well, but, having no real self-love, she can derive a sense of false self-esteem by mothering her children, who by this time may be in their thirties or fifties. She is hurt when her unsolicited advice is ignored, and so she plays the martyr role. As she ages, she wants more and more attention from her children and may become utterly unreasonable with her increasing demands. Having sought self-worth by the mother role, she knows no other way to achieve it.

— The "personality boy" who makes a career of being popular. He must be loved by everyone, for his self-worth is wrapped up not in who or what he is, but in the number of people who admire or love him. Such a man derives enormous satisfaction from his many feminine conquests. If he is rejected, he feels hurt and puzzled, for he has failed in his goal to win unconditional love (affirmation, sex, approval). His defense against seeing himself as he really is — self-doubting, unsure of himself — is to make certain that he is rejected as seldom as possible.

— The superachiever may have grown accustomed to constant adulation as a child because of good grades, superior talent, or ability to charm people. Not having known defeat, and being gifted in some way, such a person often confuses performance with character, and achievement with self-worth. One who has seldom if ever experienced failure or had to take second place often has difficulty accepting defeat graciously, and defeat in this case means not being looked up to and admired, or not being in the spotlight.

No One Ever Said It Would Be Easy

Until maturity comes, many people tend to have the naive misconception that life is going to be easy. What a mistake! Life is very complex; and it can be disappointing and sometimes very lonely. Charles Darwin's theory of organic evolution rested heavily upon the concept of "the survival of the fittest." Some people imagine that this applies only to the animal world. It also includes humans. The records are full of countless species of plant and animal life that have died out because they didn't adapt. They were dropouts in the battle for survival. And in the human struggle for survival, resilience and patient endurance are essential.

Are you waiting for something wonderful to happen to you? There is always the remote possibility that it will. You could win the Irish sweepstakes; your daydreams could materialize; yes, the good fairy could appear and make it so. But it isn't likely, is it?

The statement of Jesus, perhaps not recorded in its entirety, goes like this: "Ask, and it will be given you; seek, and you will find; knock, and it will be opened to you" (Matthew 7:7, RSV). At first it sounds almost like magic, doesn't it? Yet the idea of magical answers to prayer is not consistent with the rest of his teachings. Let's make that read (as he may well have intended): "Ask and keep asking until you discover the answers; seek and keep on seeking until you find what it is you are looking for; don't give up! Knock on every door until you find the one that opens to you, and behind which there is something worthwhile."

EMOTIONS, HEALTH, AND SELF-WORTH

Check your health. If you are lacking in drive and energy, it could be from physical as well as emotional causes: a malfunctioning thyroid, hypoglycemia (low blood sugar), a mineral imbalance, a vitamin deficiency, or a score of other causes.

At one point in my life I experienced a significant loss of energy. I took all kinds of tests. One physician thought me to be a hypochondriac, since excessive fatigue is one of the most common complaints in doctors' offices. Finally, insisting on more than a standard examination, I asked for exhaustive blood tests. The results came back indicating four or five times the normal level of lead in my system. Just because you have had a physical examination and nothing serious was discovered doesn't mean that you are well physically. Sometimes more complete blood tests are needed.

Recent studies have shown that excessive coffee drinking can play a significant part in nervousness. People who are tense and nervous should limit their coffee intake, and probably avoid it entirely, according to many authorities.

I recall a woman with severe emotional problems who did

not respond to any form of therapy. Checking with her about her diet, I discovered that because of a neurotic fear of being obese like her mother, she had for years lived on a totally inadequate diet. I could not induce her to change it. No human organism could be expected to function well on her diet. Eventually, she ended up receiving shock therapy, preferring that to the threat of gaining weight. Results were minimal. She was, incidentally, at least twelve to fifteen pounds underweight.

Share your guilt. This can be very threatening. Remember that *time does not diminish guilt.* The event may have transpired many years ago; but the sense of guilt remains *unless* you have a deep sense of having been forgiven and have forgiven yourself. I have dealt with people who have finally blurted out guilt feelings thirty and forty years old. There was something self-defeating in the lives of each one. In one there was a physical diability that defied medical science. In another, the woman kept getting fired, despite her great ability and brilliant mind. She was unconsciously punishing herself.

Shared Guilt Can Bring Relief

The longer some ancient guilt is kept concealed, the more damage it does to the personality, and the more terrible the guilt seems. Guilty secrets are very damaging to the personality and often account for continued defeat.

If you have a guilty secret, you can get relief by sharing it with an understanding, accepting minister, or with a psychologist or psychiatrist. Avoid, however, as you would the plague, a counselor who is judgmental.

There is an understandable reluctance to share areas of guilt with another. One feels ashamed, embarrassed, and vulnerable. It often seems better, for the moment, to bury the guilt. The difficulty is that it requires a sizeable amount of psychic energy to keep up the pretense. Hiding buried guilt is stress-producing, and anyone in need of a stronger self-acceptance needs all of the psychic energy he can summon.

Learn to accept love, as well as give it. It can sometimes be less demeaning or embarrassing to give than to receive. It is humbling to be on the receiving end, to be in need and seek help. To be a gracious recipient is as important as being a generous giver.

It is terrifying to be helpless, friendless, afraid, and

ashamed. A woman was flung at Jesus' feet by the Pharisees, who were seeking to trap him (John 8:3-11). She had been caught in the very act of adultery, they said. (It is interesting that no charges were brought against the man.) The law of Moses said that she should be stoned. Some in the crowd were already picking up stones for the exciting, self-righteous act of stoning the adulteress. It was a clever way of unconsciously dissipating their own guilt. "Let him who is without sin cast the first stone," Jesus said. Then he knelt and wrote in the sand with his finger. His face would have been on a level with hers.

"Let him who is without sin. . . ." There is embarrassment, confusion, and dismay in the crowd. One by one they begin to disperse. Don't look back. Look straight ahead. Urgent business elsewhere. Finally there is no crowd left — just Jesus and a crouching woman.

"Where are your accusers?" She raises her head, looks about. "They've all gone." "Neither do I condemn you; you may go now — but — look, don't keep up this way of life, because if you do, you're going to hurt yourself." That's the sense and the spirit of what he said. But more important was that look. She would remember the words more clearly later, when she relived the scene. Just now she's looking into his eyes. They are warm and friendly and searching. They are forgiving eyes, because there is love in them. No one had ever loved her this way before; and he is so relaxed, so accepting. He isn't judgmental. There's no indignation over her moral failure. She had condemned herself a hundred times, but the self-hate seemed to intensify the demand for some kind of affection, and the inner cry for someone to care — even for an hour or a night.

Later, after she had left him, she would think again and again of the scene. "He protected me from those men. They wanted to kill me! He saved me with a single sentence. I was so frightened; they were so hateful, so hideous. And some of those men I had known — intimately. And he — he was so tender, so gentle, yet strong, too.

"I will never forget those compassionate eyes. I think he liked me; no, it was more, he loved me, but in a way I've never been loved before. How could he love *me*, after all I've been? It isn't as if he didn't know. He knew! He knew without their having to tell him. He looked right into me and knew more than they could tell him. But he still liked me, accepted me, *loved* me — that's the amazing part. I don't know who he is, but I love him, in a way I've never loved anyone. I want to know him better. I'd even·like to follow him, be with him. I wonder what it would be like just to be around him.

"And strange . . . he made me like myself better. I feel better about myself. More — clean? Whole? Is that it? I feel that I could almost begin to love myself. Is that possible? He didn't condemn me. He accepted me, loved me — and now I can begin to love myself. Beautiful!"

Notes

[1]Nathaniel Branden, *The Psychology of Self-Esteem* (New York: Bantam Books, 1975).

[2]Order from Yokefellows, Inc., 19 Park Road, Burlingame, CA 94010.

9 Take the Risk!

9 Take the Risk!

Life is difficult, but vastly preferable to the alternative.

— *Gabriel Montalban*

An excessively timid monk in a monastery repeatedly avoided the assignment of delivering the chapel sermon when his turn came. Eventually, his superior ordered him to either give the sermon or spend two weeks in the kitchen. Fearfully, he took the plunge.

Standing before his fellow monks in the chapel, he was seized with terror and completely forgot his sermon. He asked, "Do you know what I am going to tell you this morning?" They shook their heads. "Neither do I, and so we will now have the benediction."

Ordered to try again on the following Sunday, he was once more frozen with fear. Finally he said, "Do you men know what I am going to tell you this morning?" They all nodded. "In that case," he said, "there is no point in my telling you. We will now have the benediction."

His superior was determined to give him one more chance. The third Sunday the frozen-faced young monk stood at the pulpit and again forgot his carefully prepared sermon. "Do you men know what I am going to tell you?" Half of them nodded, and the other half shook their heads. "In that case," said the young monk, "let those who know tell those who do not. We will now have the benediction."

Well, he made the attempt. He took the risk. Failure is not nearly so bad as living with the knowledge that we never tried.

One of the saddest, most melancholy phrases in the English language is "If only. . . ." If only I had tried; if only I had done differently; if only I had taken the risk — what a sad and desolate ring that has. And the fearful, doubting individual tends also to look ahead to the future with the same sort of morbid doubt and fear, and asks "What if. . . ?"

Take the risk of building your self-esteem! Reach out to people in love and friendship. Instead of waiting for others to greet or welcome you, reach out. Take the risk! There is no more reason for them to greet you than for you to speak first.

I was invited once to speak at a ministers' breakfast. When I arrived a bit early, seven men stood scattered about in the room in silence. Unlike most pastor's groups I have been in, these men seemed afraid and almost alienated. I discovered that they did not know each other, and each hesitated to break the ice. Although I am not an instinctive mixer or extrovert by nature, I approached one of the men and introduced myself, then I introduced him to the others. Eventually I got them, and subsequent arrivals, into little clusters where they chatted with diminishing self-consciousness. Theirs was unusual behavior for ministers, who are usually more outgoing; but it is typical of the way many people act — waiting for someone else to speak first.

What have you to lose by extending the hand of friendship? No one is going to reject you! It is a skill learned only by practice. Reading won't help you; prayer alone will not do it for you; there comes a time when you have to take the risk. Remember the "act as if" principle, and that feelings follow actions.

Risk paying compliments. Someone once said, "I have never been insulted or bored by someone paying me a compliment." If you find that receiving compliments makes you feel mildly embarrassed, then you undoubtedly find it hard to offer sincere praise. But it is a skill that can be cultivated. The compliment need not be effusive. Flowery, overdone praise sounds insincere; but everyone appreciates the quiet, sincere comment: "I love your home. It's so warm and friendly." Or, "What a lovely dress," or whatever.

Jesus validated this spirit of openly expressing love with the general principle: "Give, and it will be given to you . . ." (Luke 6:38). If you who hunger for expressions of appreciation and love will launch out on a program of giving approval and sincere praise, you will begin to receive. Don't stand there waiting to be liked and approved! Get into motion! You feel insincere? No, what you mean is that you feel awkward, and that's because you haven't practiced it often enough or long enough so that it seems natural. Any skill or art requires diligent practice.

Risk making mistakes. Is it fatal if you blunder occasionally? A friend of mine, the head of a large business concern, once said ruefully, "I was forty years old before I had sense enough to say, 'I don't know.' Finally I had a stroke of sanity and learned to say, 'I don't know, but I'll find out for you.' " The fear of appearing ignorant, of making a mistake, of not having all the answers, had limited his effectiveness for years.

You will gain in self-esteem if you gather your courage and admit that you — like everyone else — make mistakes. One man I know said that his fear of making mistakes and of appearing wrong had paralyzed him for years. He formed the habit of saying to himself, "So I blew it; big deal!" At first, he said, he felt insincere and self-conscious when he said it. In time he began to feel comfortable with the idea that it is all right to make mistakes.

Related to this is the difficulty most people have in saying, "I'm sorry." A friend of mine said that his wife of forty years had never once admitted to being wrong, nor had she ever said, "I'm sorry." This is strong evidence of a terribly weak self-esteem. Those who like and accept themselves have the courage — and wisdom — to say, "I'm sorry; I was wrong," when it seems indicated. Only the brash or self-rejecting pretend to be always right.

A song has it, "Love means never having to say you're sorry," but this is a terribly false concept. Love — love for oneself and love for another — means *being willing* to say, "I'm sorry."

Risk complaining when it is justified. A woman told me that during an operation involving a complex blood transfusion, she felt rather severe pain. The physician told her that this was normal. After he left the room, the pain continued. "I'm not normally a complainer," she said, "but I just felt that something was wrong. I hated to bother the physician who had assured me that everything was normal, but I sent my husband to ask him to come back. He rather impatiently examined the needle in my arm, then with considerable alarm said, 'My word, this needle has been put in wrong.' " She had lost a large amount of blood, and the doctor told her husband later that she would have died if she had not complained.

I find it a bit difficult to complain, as do many people. I prefer to put up with a great deal in preference to "making a scene." But increasingly I practice quietly, or otherwise, insisting upon being treated fairly. With considerable reluctance I once sent a tough steak back to the chef. I was practicing insisting on being treated fairly.

Complaints need not be expressed in anger. They can be stated with quiet insistence.

My wife, Isobel, has the ability to insist gently but firmly that people perform as they are supposed to. She doesn't make a scene over it, but does stand her ground. My inborn tendency is to react in one of two ways: either to submit to the mistreatment, or react with excessive anger or indignation. Neither is appropriate, of course.

The individual who does not have sufficient self-esteem will put up with almost anything, particularly if the person behind the desk or counter, or wearing a uniform (officer, conductor, street-sweeper, petty clerk) seems authoritative. It requires practice to stand one's ground firmly. It need not be a contest of wills; it may involve nothing more than a quiet, firm, courteous insistence on having the matter settled properly.

Risk being embarrassed. Few people enjoy the confusion and self-reproach that may follow some severe embarrassment. Yet how much we miss by never running a reasonable risk.

I could probably be described as "a cautious plunger." The caution is because I don't want to look bad or fail or be embarrassed; the plunger part stems from the desire to see more, do more, and experience more. I saw this in operation once in the Hashemite Kingdom of the Jordan. I was on my way with a friend to Petra "the rose-red city half as old as time," long before there was a good road from Jerusalem to that part of the desert, where once the Nabateans had held sway. We spent the night near Petra at Eljib, inside a walled Arab Legion army post.

The lonely soldiers were friendly, and we talked at great length. I admired their beautiful Arabian horses, and one of the men asked if I would like to ride. I had ridden a great deal as a boy, and a few times since. I said, "Yes, I think I have always had a secret desire to ride with the Arab Legion."

They had a great deal of fun outfitting me in flowing robe and Arab headdress. I mounted, with a dozen or so others, and together we galloped wildly off over the hills. As we swung in a wide circle and started our return to the fort, my fellow riders reined in and stopped. My horse kept on going. I pulled hard on the reins, but there was no response. Behind me I heard hilarious laughter. This was going to be embarrassing. I knew how to ride, but this horse just didn't seem to understand my particular technique. Eventually I succeeded in getting him to turn in smaller and smaller circles, and at last he came to a very reluctant stop at the entrance to the fort. My robed friends were rolling on the ground with uncontrolled hilarity. I felt pretty sheepish. Then I dismounted and examined the bridle. The soldiers waited expectantly. I discovered that they had played a joke on me. My horse had no bridle. There was only a simple halter with improvised reins. With no bit in its mouth, of course, the horse was uncontrollable.

The soldiers hadn't had so much fun in years, they told me. After a while I was able to join them in laughing about it. At least I had "ridden with the Arab Legion."

I have been embarrassed a thousand times by taking risks; but it has never been fatal. Without risking mistakes no one ever makes very much progress. A child learning to walk runs the risk of falling. The student runs the risk of failure. The job applicant risks rejection. A couple planning marriage has only two chances in three or four of success. Life is a risk! God took a risk with Adam and Eve.

The Old Testament tells the story of some lepers who saved a city from starvation (2 Kings 7). Samaria was besieged and the people were starving. Four lepers sitting at the city gate made a bold decision. They agreed among themselves that they would slip out through one of the city gates and approach the enemy who surrounded the city. They reasoned, "Why do we sit here till we die? If we say, 'Let us enter the city,' the famine is in the city, and we shall die there; and if we sit here, we die also. So now come, let us go over to the camp of the Syrians; if they spare our lives we shall live, and if they kill us we shall but die" (vv. 3,4, RSV).

Upon approaching the Syrian camp, they found it abandoned. "For the Lord had made the army of the Syrians hear the sound of chariots, and of horses, the sound of a great army, so that they said to one another, 'Behold the king of Israel has hired against us the kings of the Hittites and the kings of Egypt to come upon us.' So they fled . . . for their lives" (vv. 6,7, RSV). They took a chance, and saved their lives.

Everyone hates rejection. No one enjoys job hunting or asking for a raise, and few people can ask a favor with ease. As one's self-esteem increases, it becomes easier. Most of us find it far easier to extend a helping hand than to ask for help. The one offering assistance is in a superior position. He is the giver. The one soliciting help is placed in the inferior position, as supplicant, and thus runs the possible risk of rejection. We all dislike hearing the word *no*.

I had transferred from a very small university to Columbia University after my second year and was awed by the vastness of both the university and of New York City itself. I still felt like the eighteen-year-old hick that I was. The entrance exams frightened me half out of my mind. I had never taken that kind of a test and I knew I would flunk it, and I did.

Thinking it over the next day, I realized what I had done wrong. I had foolishly spent too much time stewing over questions to which I did not know the answer, instead of going on to the next one. I asked the instructor for a chance to retake the test and was told that it was never done. I was crushed. The next day I decided to go back and try again, though I was terrified of the rejection I was expecting would come. The instructor refused to reconsider. Four times I went back, until finally, to get rid of me, he gave me another chance. This time I was less frightened and ended up with a score in the upper brackets. So much for overriding one's fear. Desperation is a great cure for cowardice.

But I can recall hundreds of instances when my impulse to ask, or to reach out to someone, has been thwarted by a natural diffidence; and I think with regret of the many times when, had I taken the risk, I might have accomplished more both for myself and for others.

As indicated in an earlier chapter, many people can overcome the reluctance to say no when it is appropriate, by learning to say, at first, "Yes, I'd be glad to, but. . . ." This permits the use of a yes instead of a no and allows time for the mind to come up with a suitable reason. Since I have a lifelong tendency to say yes to any and all requests, and thus overcommit myself both in terms of time and energy, I discovered that I had to use such a device until I could find a better one. For some absurd reason I always felt that I should give a detailed explanation of why I couldn't comply with the request. If my date book had a blank space in it, I nearly always gave in. Occasionally people would ask, "What are you doing Tuesday night?" I felt, like all overcompliant people, that I had to answer that stupid question. I recall having people look over my shoulder as I examined my date book. Finally I learned to reply to such questions, "What do you have in mind?" And if the request or invitation did not appeal to me, I could reply, "I'd love to, but I am tied up that night." Sometimes I felt guilty about saying I was busy, when actually all I had in mind was staying home, perhaps for the first night that month. It eventually dawned on me that it was no one's business what I was doing; that if I was busy with my family, or with the TV, or reading, or simply resting for a change, I did not have to give a detailed explanation.

Take the risk of asking for what you want. About sixty-five percent of the population fears to make simple, legitimate requests. Often they do not receive because they do not ask.

A friend of mine — a gentle, warm, loving person — was seated on a plane next to a man reading a newspaper. He had not had time to buy his own paper before boarding the plane and very much wanted to borrow his seat-mate's paper. He said it took him half an hour to get up the courage to ask, "If you're finished with your paper, may I see it?" He knew in his mind that no normal person could refuse such a sensible request; yet some ancient fear made it difficult for him to ask.

I said, "Did you find it hard to make requests of your parents?" "Yes, my father was very stern, and mother was too busy with seven kids to respond to my needs; I guess I just learned not to ask for anything. I've always found it difficult."

"What was your father's general response when you asked for something?" He smiled to cover the pain of an ancient hurt. "Dad was always grumpy and very demanding. He offered no praise, only criticism. I just learned to shut up and stay out of his way as much as possible. I suppose that's how I learned never to ask, and not even to expect very much from life." Thus are our adult habits formed in childhood, in relation to parents and other authority figures.

Risk expressing love. Charles McCabe, a San Francisco columnist, wrote about his difficulty in expressing love. He told of the death of a friend:

> We had gone through quite a few things together. Yet, had he thought of me at all during his last days of illness, there is no way he could have known that I not only liked him but rather loved

him. I do not know how common this affliction is, this inability
to express love. I know that it has been with me nearly all my
life, and has caused me many moments of regret. . . .

I doubt if my mother ever kissed me more than a couple of
times in the years that I can remember. As I grew up, disapproval was vocal, even strident, and was the general tone of
social intercourse.

When you did something that warranted approval, you
were rewarded with silence. . . . Not to be harried, not to feel
constantly the chastening whip, was a reward.

Gushing was a great sin in my house. It has remained so,
though there is a wealth of example to tell me of the folly of this
reflex. . . . I would like to go on the housetops and shout
shamelessly the names of the persons I love. And I would, of
course, except I feel that it would somehow be an accusation of
myself. Therefore I could not do it.[1]

He thinks of this conditioned response as irreversible, and
perhaps it is in his case, though I doubt it. If one is sufficiently
motivated, it is possible to unlearn the negative and acquire the
positive responses. Required are motivation, practice, and patience.

Ellie had great difficulty expressing love, for she had never
been loved as a child, at least not in a manner that she could
accept. How she learned not only to express love, but to take
charge of an empty life is an interesting story. I quote from her
account in some detail because it points up some important
principles.

I was born into a wealthy family, at the top of the social ladder.
From infancy to the age of nineteen I lacked nothing that
money could buy. The only thing I remember wanting was for
someone to love me. As a child I would go to my elegantly
decorated room, shut the door and cry because I hurt so badly. I
felt all mixed-up because I could see all the "things" around me,
but it didn't help the unloved, unwanted feeling inside. All the
things they bought me — clothes, cars, private schools, sum-
mer camps, trips — never bought me happiness; and this made
me feel guilty, for I had been told that all those material things
should make me happy. They didn't. I knew I was not worthwhile, no good, because all the material things I had didn't
make me feel good inside.

After a marriage failure, she and her children were supported
lavishly by her father. She continues:

Through one man who took an interest in me, and Yokefellows,

I was exposed to the word "fulfilling." I began a long and still-continuing search for the meaning of that word in my life. When my father suddenly cut off my support, I was forced to go to work. I had not been trained for anything. I had zero self-value and zero confidence. I felt I was a no-good, unlovable, worthless person, emotionally bankrupt.

God and I together found a job as a salesclerk in a children's store. For the first six months I didn't get any satisfaction from my work. I felt anyone could do what I was doing. Slowly I was given added responsibility. I became assistant manager, then finally manager and buyer. With this promotion, I began to realize what the word "fulfilling" meant. Life suddenly had a new meaning. I had some worth. Life became more difficult in some ways, with new responsibilities. There was the conflict between job versus motherhood. I deeply desire to have the freedom to be a full-time mother. This is still a conflict; but life is more fulfilling, because I have worked very hard to change my outlook from a negative one to one that is more positive. This change from negative to positive has taught me to enjoy life more, and I find that now I want to reach out to hurting human beings, to love people who don't love themselves. I know now that Christ had put in me the strength that makes me a winner.

The changing force in my life was one man and one woman. They saw things in me I couldn't see, and took time to tell me the value they saw in me. They wanted my company and introduced me to their personal friends, which showed me I had some worth. The man looked me in the eye and told me what I had going for me, and added, "I'll stand with you and we will lick this thing together." I felt that if this man and his wife could give me so much — and love me so much — that I was going to make it. It wasn't an overnight thing, but I climb a little every day. . . .

One day it dawned on me that loving others gave me a fulfillment that work couldn't. I decided to take this new love and put it to work in the store which I managed. It has worked! There is occasional fear and discouragement, but they do not dominate my life. Positive feelings are in the majority. . . . This all came about because two people cared enough about me to love me.

At first Ellie couldn't love herself, of course, because she had never felt loved. Thus she had no love to give to anyone else. With growing self-acceptance and self-love she began to feel not only fulfillment but the impulse to reach out and love others.

Run the risk of being your true self. Your real self may not be the person with whom you are familiar, but someone entirely different. If you don't know who you are, the first step is to find out.

In a large church where I was conducting a weekend retreat I had occasion to work closely with the delightful associate minister. He seemed to be greatly admired and loved by the members and told me that he was quite happy in his work. He enjoyed being an associate, preferring not to be burdened with too much administrative work.

His wife, a charming and beautiful young woman, was not happy, however. She revealed her great unhappiness over the fact that her husband was not the senior minister. "I want my husband to be top dog," she said. "I can't accept anything but the number-one slot."

They lived in a beautiful home and had several lovely children. She had every outward reason to be supremely happy, but was made utterly miserable by the neurotic need to be "on top."

In a lengthy counseling session I discovered the basic reason for her unhappiness. Her parents had wanted a boy. For the first ten or twelve years of her life she tried to act like a boy in order to win her parents' approval. "I have never felt okay as a woman. My parents didn't accept me as a girl, and now I can't accept myself as a woman. I did everything I could to win every first place, to be always number one, because if I didn't, I felt utterly worthless. Being on top is important to me, since I have so little self-worth."

I said, "If your husband were the senior minister of this church, would that satisfy you *completely?*" She said thoughtfully, "No, I don't think so. I'd want him to be the senior minister of the *largest* church, and this isn't." She admitted in further discussion that even then she would want him to be the senior minister of the largest church in the state, and probably ultimately, in the nation. She laughed at the absurdity of her escalating ambition. "It's ridiculous, isn't it? What can I do about it?"

I said, "First of all, you have no real identity of your own. You tried to be a boy, and of course you couldn't. You tried to be first in everything to win parental approval, but that could never make up for your parents' neurotic need to have a boy. You will never win the game you're playing, because you are pursuing the wrong goal. Make it your goal to find out who *you* are. You must be an individual, with your own identity, apart from your husband."

"How do I start?"

"There are numerous ways. One is to find a job, apart from the kind of work your husband does, where you can succeed in winning approval for your work. Each small success will build confidence. Eventually you will discover that being approved for what you *do* is not as satisfying as being loved and admired for who you *are*. Job success is like four-by-four props put under a building to hold it up until the genuine concrete foundation can be put under it. Props are not to be despised, but they are to be recognized for what they are: temporary supports for a faltering ego. A real foundation is the awareness that you are a worthwhile person *just as you are*. With your background it will take time, but it can be done." However, I warned her, "You must give up completely the idea of making your identity and happiness hinge upon your husband's advancement. Be a person in your own right. Incidentally, he will undoubtedly succeed far better when you are fulfilled and happy, and not pushing him."

Risk getting to the root of your problem. If you are seriously troubled by low self-worth and if deep feelings of inferiority have prevented you from getting the most from life, get into therapy. Sometimes "talk therapy," where you simply sit and talk with a therapist, can be effective; but usually a deep-seated sense of inferiority requires something more than talking and reading books; for books and talk therapy speak to the intellect, whereas the problem nearly always lies deeply buried in the unconscious mind.

How does one get into the unconscious? Certainly not by intellectualizing, or any simple standard approach. Often an intensive therapy group can provide a solution; but do not look for a quick cure for a lifelong problem. I think of one highly intelligent woman, functioning well as wife and mother and in her work, who has for twelve years been in an intensive Yokefellow group that I lead. Another has belonged for six years. They believe that emotional and spiritual growth is an open-ended process.

In-Depth Therapy, dealing with primal feelings, is another option for those who are highly motivated. In the first two years that this intensive therapy was offered at the Burlingame Counseling Center,[2] people came from fifteen states prepared to stay three weeks or longer for daily sessions. Nearly all were Christians, and most had previously experienced some other form of therapy. These are not "sick" people, but hurting persons who want more out of life and are willing to search diligently for solutions to life's deepest problems.

It suddenly occurred to me one day that there is one interesting facet of the story of the prodigal son that I had never investigated thoroughly. Everyone is familiar with this best-known of Jesus' parables: the rebellious son of a loving father impetuously demands his share of the inheritance. (It is interesting to note that the father accedes to his unreasonable request.)

The son leaves home and in some distant country dissipates his inheritance in riotous living. (And with prostitutes, his elder brother bitterly complains later.) The country suffers a severe depression, and the only work the destitute wanderer can find is that of tending swine. In his hunger he is tempted to eat the husks that are fed to the pigs. He remembers that the servants in his father's house eat better than he, and he resolves to return to his father and ask to be treated like a servant. He rehearses his humble speech of repentance and starts the long homeward journey.

The father sees him "afar off." (Had he been watching that road day after day?) Seeing his son in the distance, the father rushes out to greet him, and with effusive expressions of love smothers the young man's speech of repentance. He embraces his son and, summoning the servants, commands them to spread the good news to all the friends and neighbors that his long-lost son has returned.

"His father said to the slaves, 'Quick! Bring the finest robe in the house and put it on him. And a jeweled ring for his finger; and shoes! And kill the calf we have in the fattening pen. We must celebrate with a feast, for this son of mine was dead and has returned to life. He was lost and is found.' So the party began" (Luke 15:11-32, *The Living Bible*).

We rejoice with the father that his son has returned and that he feels no need to reprimand him, or even to express the hope that he has learned his lesson. We can understand the invitation to friends and neighbors, the joyous banquet, the fatted calf, and the robe; but the jeweled ring! Why a *ring*? There is no necessity for a piece of jewelry at this point. The son neither deserves nor asks for it. He has asked for nothing, and receives a joyous homecoming celebration. What does he need a ring for? Why did Jesus add that detail to the story?

I think the answer is fairly simple. The father's welcome, his unstated forgiveness, his joy over the return, the robe, and the banquet represent God's limitless love and forgiveness. The ring symbolizes his ineffable, unbelievable *grace*, a gift that has nothing to do with worthiness, with being either righteous nor unrighteous, saint or sinner. His grace is offered us not because we are *good*, but because we are *his*. We do not feel worthy; he sees us as possessing supreme worth. We cannot love ourselves properly; he declares that we are loved with "an everlasting love." There *must* be something truly wonderful about us if he can love and accept us so readily.

What he loves about us is that portion of himself he has planted deep within — soul, spirit, God-self — and he wants us to love this immortal Self as he does.

He longs for our return from our wandering. Whether the return be motivated by humility born of despair, or by sheer love for the Source of all love, he awaits us and gladly offers all of the limitless resources of the kingdom.

Notes

[1]*San Francisco Chronicle*, September 16, 1975.
[2]Associated with Yokefellows, Inc., 19 Park Road, Burlingame, CA 94010.

APPENDIXES

APPENDIX A

Primal Feelings

I first discovered what psychologist Arthur Janov terms "Primal Therapy" in a therapy group I was leading years ago, before I was familiar with the term. Several of the group members were very much out of touch with their deep emotions. One of them, a young married woman in her early thirties, had been in a mental institution a number of times for brief periods.

"My parents did their best," she said, "but they were unfeeling persons who didn't want me to express any emotions. They were determined that I should be a 'good girl,' which meant being compliant, obedient, never angry, always polite — in other words, a sweet little robot without feelings. The worst sin in their book was to express anger or even irritation. God didn't like naughty little girls. So I buried all feelings in order to win their love and approval. I guess a kid needs that approval so much that no price is too great.

"In my twenties I had so much anxiety from repressing all of my deeper emotions that they sent me to a psychiatrist. It didn't do any good. Talking *about* my feelings proved a waste of time. I now know that I desperately needed to *feel* my emotions, not just discuss them. Eventually I cracked up from all the boiling, turbulent, unexpressed frustration and anger inside me, and they sent me to a psychiatric hospital. When they locked me up in my little room, I felt so relieved I began to beat on the walls and scream. Those screams came right up from my toes, wave after wave of emotions I had wanted to express all my life — rage, frustration, anger — you name it. It felt so good to be able to express those long-buried feelings, but I had gotten out only a few full-bodied screams before two or three attendants rushed in, shouting, "Here, here! You can't do that. Now quiet down!" Then they gave me a massive injection of something and I slept for eighteen hours. Those poor, misguided psychiatric nurses and doctors didn't know that all I needed was a sound-proofed room where I could scream out a lifetime of repressed feelings. I was in and out of that place several times. Eventually they found a balance of antidepressants and tranquilizers which kept me from flipping out periodically; but I was still bottled up and rigid, fearful of something unknown. I'd have to phone my husband at work five or ten times a day just to hear the sound of his voice in order to get relief from the terrifying, nameless anxiety and dread.

"Then, in this group I discovered the answer, and my healing began." She smiled. "I still have some more work to do on this, but I am experiencing release, and I know that this is the answer."

Phyllis had been a baby-faced, unresponsive, emotionally deadened person, barely surviving on a monumental mixture of drugs that kept her from flipping into psychosis but did not permit her to feel anything except the diffused depression that results from shutting down on all emotions.

Her healing began in an experimental vein. The psychiatrist she saw periodically warned me that one should not probe too deeply into her feelings lest a Pandora's box of terrible fears and memories be released. He was content to let her remain an emotionally rigid, fearful, half-dead woman whose greatest hope was to remain "sane" enough to avoid going back to a mental hospital.

At that time I knew nothing of what is now called Primal Therapy, or in some circles, "the healing of memories," but felt led to follow up on a deep conviction. It was that depression is not an emotion, but the shutting down on all, or almost all, feelings. I knew that instead of opening a Pandora's box of "evil emotions," I could help her by making her aware of her feelings. Most emotionally troubled people need to be given permission to express their long-buried feelings of fear and hurt that have been shut off since early childhood.

Relying on some inner urge rather than experience, which I did not have at that point, I had her do some deep breathing for several minutes, then regressed her to childhood and told her to float around for a bit between ages three and six. By utilizing some other techniques since refined through thousands of hours of experience, she was triggered into a series of ear-splitting screams. She directed them at her mother first: rage, fear, indignation, pain, hate. This placid, frozen-faced young woman suddenly became a feeling person for the first time in her life, except for the brief moments when she had screamed in the mental hospital. When her rage at mother seemed exhausted, she began to scream at daddy, only now it was a mixture of hurt and a longing for daddy to love her, cuddle her, talk to her. She continued until she was completely exhausted. Then she began to sob almost uncontrollably. These were primal sobs, in the voice of a little girl, tears of hurt and loneliness she had never been allowed to shed, for crying was as great a sin as anger in her home.

"What a relief it was to get those screams and tears out at that first session," she said. "I knew there was much more down there, and it did come out in later private sessions, but I had never experienced such relief in my entire life as I did when I was allowed to scream my anger and hurt. I knew right then that I could get rid of all those pills I was living on." Ultimately, she was able to function without her tranquilizers and antidepressants.

Subsequently she had between forty and fifty hours of individual therapy, letting out the accumulated Pain of her thirty-two years. Seven years of rather intensive "talk therapy" had been able to accomplish little more than stabilizing her as an emotionally depressed robot.

Can you remember some of the humiliation endured at the hands of your parents, peers, or playmates? The demands, criticism, scoldings, whippings, shouts? If you can recall half a dozen such instances, you can be sure there are hundreds buried deep in your unconscious mind. We have listened to adults who thought they had a reasonably good childhood, as they sobbed, pleaded, cringed, or begged for a morsel of love and understanding.

In 1930 Freud wrote of "the error of supposing that ordinary forgetting signified destruction or annihilation of the memory trace. . . . Everything survives in some way or other and is capable under certain conditions of being brought to light again . . . when regression extends back far enough."[1]

It is not uncommon in In-Depth Therapy for the birth experience to be relived in infinite detail, and, where birth has involved an unusual amount of pain and fear for the infant, reliving this experience has often proved very therapeutic.

We now know experientially that nothing is ever lost, nothing completely forgotten. Waiting to be recalled are the memories of all that has ever happened to us. The erosion of the years does not destroy any experience or event: the infant screaming for his bottle, the anguish of being born, the embarrassment experienced on that first date, the panic at being left at kindergarten, the shame of being ridiculed by other children, or the uncounted nights of terror when left alone in a dark room. The mind is an incredibly sensitive photographic plate on which everything has been recorded with infinite fidelity. A very few of these memories are available to recall. More than ninety-nine out of a hundred childhood memories, with all the feelings surrounding them, are filed away in the unconscious mind.

But unlike pictures filed away in a cabinet, these thousands of pain-laden memories are exerting a profound influence on our lives today. They color our attitudes, and distort our ideas. Every adult relationship is in some degree affected by those childhood experiences and the primal Pain that colors them.

Randy was a pleasant, nice-looking young man in his early twenties. Slightly over six feet tall, he had a ready smile that masked a seething mass of turbulent emotions. There had been two older brothers who played together. Randy, nicknamed "Shrimp" when he was little, was never allowed to tag along. "My younger sister Alice never had to do anything in order to get love. She was cuddled and praised, while I sat across the room and looked on enviously. My older brothers were good at everything. I couldn't read as fast as they could, or do math problems as well. In fact, they did everything well and I did everything poorly. So dad yelled at me, and mother criticized me. I did everything wrong. Dad beat me so hard I was sure he was going to kill me."

In his first primal session, lasting two hours, Randy went right to the core of his hurt. Like most people in primals, he was on a "split screen," reliving his ancient Pain with one part of his mind, but conscious that I was in the room with him. From time to time he would open his eyes and discuss his feelings, then go back into his childhood hurts. There is no chronology to childhood hurts; scenes may flash on the screen from age three along with painful events at age five or seven, or at three months. These are not "remembered" but "relived," with as much intensity as the original experience.

Randy began, in a little boy's voice, to talk to his father. "Daddy, I love you; please don't hit me, daddy; I love you. Please be nice to me, daddy; don't yell at me. Please love me, just be nice to me, daddy. I want you to hold me, daddy. Don't hit me. . . . Why don't you take me fishing like you do Freddie and Jack? I want to be with you, daddy. You scare me, daddy. I know I'm no good. I'm bad. I'm awful bad. I do everything wrong, but can't you love me just a little? I know my grades are bad, daddy, but I can't think good. Everybody does good, and I do bad. I'm just no good, and you hate me; but daddy, please love me. I love *you*, daddy. . . ." A long silence, then a scream: "Daddy! Don't kill me! Don't kill me! I'll try to be better."

He opened his eyes and said, "Daddy wasn't trying to kill me, of course, but it felt like it. He was just whipping me, I suppose, but it hurt so bad I was sure he would kill me. I was a rotten speller, and he'd yell at me when I got a word wrong. He'd use flash cards to help us with math, and my brothers always got everything right. I was so scared of him I couldn't think, and he'd shout, 'Get it right, *stupid!* Get it right! You can do better!' Then I'd really freeze up." He closed his eyes and went back down into his hurting childhood. After a few moments of guidance from me he went to another point of pain:

"Daddy will hate me! So will everyone else. Can't they see I need them? I love them. I want to be with them. I want to go fishing with you, daddy, and to the movies, and the ball game. I know I'm little, but can't you take me just once? . . . You boys tell me to go play with the girls. I don't have any friends. I must be bad. Sometimes mommy is nice. Mommy! Save me from daddy! Don't let him kill me! Don't tell him I was bad; don't tell him! He'll hit me. . . . I'm always making mistakes. I don't do *anything* right. I'm bad. I'm just no good. Everybody hates me. What am I going to do? I want you to love me, daddy. Please? Please, daddy! Please?" Then followed long, anguished sobs, stifled through the years, but as fresh as the day the little boy felt rejected and worthless.

A typical session may last two hours, sometimes longer. Since no two persons have had the same childhood experiences and because each individual has a different defense system, there is no way to estimate the precise number of hours required to get the hurts out. However, many people manage to discharge enough Pain in daily sessions over a period of three weeks to make life seem radically different. Others, whose schedules do not permit daily sessions, have primal sessions for two or more hours a week for a total of thirty to sixty hours.

Most of the several hundred people who have come for In-Depth Therapy at the Burlingame Counseling Center have previously had other forms of therapy. One woman, typical of many, had worked with a highly competent psychiatrist for six years. Though she functioned as a normal person, she could feel the stirring of some ancient, undiscovered hurt deep within, and it interfered with her peace of mind. Neither she nor her psychiatrist could account for the fact that, though she was an affectionate person, she was sexually frigid. In her third or fourth hour of In-Depth therapy she began to exhibit intense anxiety and, would say, intermittently, "It can't be! It can't be! I must be imagining this." Over a period of a week or more in daily sessions she relived the experience of having been raped as a young girl, and later molested by a relative. Both events were relived, a bit at a time, with all of the intense physical and emotional pain of the original events. After one session she said, "That just couldn't have happened. It's ridiculous. I would have remembered."

I recorded the next session and let her listen to it later. She listened in amazement, then said, "No, that actually happened. No one could fake those screams and that anguish." During three weeks of In-Depth Therapy she dealt with those traumatic events and many other childhood hurts. After returning to her home in another state, she wrote that not only the relationship with her husband, but with both her parents, had improved immeasurably. The vast, nameless dread and anxiety were gone.

There is nothing fundamentally wrong with any of us except childhood hurts. Many people who come for In-Depth Therapy tell us, "I had a pretty good childhood. My parents loved me." In many cases they report, after therapy, "I never knew how much hurt and damage loving parents can cause; and I can see now that I am doing the same thing to my own children."

Original sin, as I have come to view it after listening for countless hours to primal hurts, is not simply the sin of Adam and Eve; it is the sin (failure, misguided love, ignorance) of our parents and other authority figures. We fail because our parents failed, and they were faulty parents in some degree because their parents did not give them the unconditional, mature love they needed. That failure can be traced back to Adam and Eve, or whomever they represent. We are the victims of the corporate guilt of society. God can forgive us not only because he is a loving Father, but because he knows why we malfunction; and whether the defect in us manifests itself in the form of bank robbery, malice, lust, materialism, homosexuality, or a generalized diffused anxiety, it is because we were malformed in infancy and childhood. I say this, not in an effort to help anyone avoid responsibility, but to place the responsibility where it truly belongs: on a warped and sick society. Our individual responsibility is to recognize ourselves for the defective personalities we are, but without undue blame or self-hate. We did not decide to be the way we are any more than did the apostle Paul who said, "I don't understand myself at all, for I really want to do what is right, but I can't. I do what I don't want to — what I hate. . . . But I can't help myself, because I'm no longer doing it. It is sin inside me that is stronger than I am that makes me do these evil things" (Romans 7:15,17, *The Living Bible*).

We must avoid the tendency to shrug off sin as though it doesn't matter, and the equally false attitude that declares, "It's all my fault. I'm guilty, wrong, evil, and must take the blame."

This type of therapy has been thoroughly explained by Dr. Arthur Janov in a number of his excellent books.[2] He has apparently dealt with many people who have been damaged by a rigid, legalistic, authoritarian religion. Perhaps for this reason and conceivably because of his own orientation, he sees no particular need for religion or religious values. (The director of a large mental hospital once said, "Everyone in this institution is here because of either parents, bad religion, or bad sex, or a combination of all three.") Although In-Depth Therapy does not deal specifically with religious values, the therapists at the Burlingame Counseling Center are religiously oriented, and feel that all healing, physical or emotional, is of God. A therapist or physician is simply an agent of God, the source of all healing.

Someone at a retreat asked me if I could give biblical authority for dealing with primal feelings. I said, "I don't recall the precise passage, but it is in the chapter just after the one which authorizes a surgeon to remove a diseased appendix." Unfortunately, the reliving of ancient hurts and the discharging of the attendant anxiety surrounding those hurts are immeasurably more complex than an appendectomy. The cost is about the same and the results can be equally dramatic.

Occasionally, someone comes up with the question: "Since those things happened long ago in childhood, why not just trust God and move ahead? We're adults now, not children. Why not live in the present, without digging up all that garbage?" The problem is that, though the event is in the past, the Pain is in the person now. Time does not diminish either guilt or childhood hurts.

Another question sometimes asked is, "Is hypnosis used? If not, how do you get a person to reexperience events of twenty or forty years ago?" Hypnosis is not used. The subject is not "in someone's power." A portion of the mind is aware of what is being said and is "listening in." The adult part of the mind is hearing what the child is experiencing and expressing.

"It sounds scary. I wouldn't want to try that!" If you are living a fruitful, fulfilling life, wonderful! There is no need for a happy person, living without undue anxiety or tension, to experience any kind of therapy. As for the "scary" part, no one who has undertaken an initial experience at our center has ever said, "That was too frightening; I don't want any more." The standard reaction is, "How soon can I come back for more?"

The individuals who come for In-Depth Therapy are, with few exceptions, thought of by their friends and associates as perfectly normal people. Most of the subjects are simply aware that "there is something down there" that prevents them from being as fully effective as they wish; or, as one brilliant educator put it, "By all standards, I am a highly successful individual. But I sense a vague, diffused 'something' inside that causes me to overreact with my children, and with my wife. I am highly successful, but I am not all that happy. There's something 'down there' in the subterranean chambers of my personality that needs to come out." He discovered it in In-Depth Therapy and relived that unsatisfactory segment of his childhood. His wife wrote later, "It's thrilling to see him react to our children as a parent instead of fighting with them like a spoiled kid; and since I've gotten a lot of my own hurts out in the same way, I can relate to him as a husband, instead of the way I related to my Dad, with a mixture of fear, love, and hate."

Notes

[1] Sigmund Freud, *Civilization and Its Discontents*, trans. Joan Riviere (New York: Doubleday & Co., Inc., 1958).

[2] *The Primal Scream* (New York: Dell Publishing, 1970); *The Primal Revolution* (New York: Simon & Schuster, Inc., 1972); *The Feeling Child* (New York: Simon & Schuster, Inc., 1973).

APPENDIX B

Some Parental "Put-downs"

These are additional parental "put-downs," selected from hundreds I have collected:

If I've told you once, I've told you a thousand times!
What in the world are we going to *do* with you?
Why do you *do* those stupid things?
Oh, for heaven's *sake!*
You know better than that!
You should have been a *boy*.
What did I ever do to deserve *this?*
How many times have I *told* you . . . ?
You'll never amount to a *thing!*
Hold your *shoulders* back!
Stand up straight!
Can't you be more careful!
What's the *matter* with you?
Did you *hear* me?
Don't *bother* me!
Shut up!
Why can't you grow up?
Use your head!
After all I've done for you!
Don't you have any pride?
You'll be the death of me yet.
Go to your room till you're sorry.
I'm disappointed in you!
Money doesn't grow on trees.
What makes you so *stupid!*
You can do better than that!
What did you do *that* for?
Good grief, look what you did!
I'm going to slap your face if you do that again!
Why can't you be more like your sister (brother)?
Why do you get into so much trouble?
Why can't you be more like other boys?
You make me sick!
You're going to come to a bad end!
Stop biting your nails.

Don't be so silly.
You shouldn't *feel* that way.
Can't you do *anything* right?
Would that please Jesus?
God can see you wherever you are!
God doesn't love naughty little girls.
What are you doing, for heaven's sake?
How dumb can you get?
What will the *neighbors* say?
You *owe* it to us.
Keep quiet. Shut up.
You don't know what you're talking about.
Get out of my way!
Quit crying or I'll slap you again!
Why don't you smile?
What a dumb thing to do!
I'm disappointed in you.
You're bad.
Hold your stomach in!
Look at this room!
Don't talk back to me!
Why don't you say something? You never talk!
Didn't you hear me when I called?
Are you deaf?
When will you stop being so clumsy?

Parents can be driven beyond endurance by frustrating, irritating, exasperating children. They often feel a mixture of self-pity and anger that children can be so demanding, so unbelievably awful. It's not easy being a parent.

But right now focus on any of those parental shouts, screams, and sighs of exasperation that pushed *your* red buttons as a child. Perhaps only a few will ring a bell, perhaps none; but since children are so uniformly given to being unreasonable — by parental standards — your parents (or authority figures) expressed anger or frustration by tone of voice, body language, or facial expression. It is not only that put-downs can be so terribly devastating to the child; it is that so often parents give ten or twenty criticisms for every positive bit of affirmation. If it could have been reversed, with ten expressions of love and affirmation for every shout of exasperation, it would not have been so destructive.

Try to avoid blaming your parents or yourself. There is no

one to blame. We are all trying to do our best nearly all the time. That our best is so often pitifully inadequate is simply part of the human condition. Call it original sin, corporate guilt, or human fallibility, it all adds up to the same thing: "All have sinned . . ." (Romans 3:23).

And the antidote for that is found in the glorious truth that "God sent the Son into the world . . . that the world might be saved through him" (John 3:17, RSV).

APPENDIX C

Psychological Test to Determine the
Degree of Your Self-Acceptance

True___ False___ 1. I received from my parents about all the love I needed.

True___ False___ 2. I am no more self-conscious than the average person.

True___ False___ 3. I seldom feel terribly critical of people.

True___ False___ 4. I have about as many friends as I would like.

True___ False___ 5. It doesn't bother me much when people I know do something really stupid.

True___ False___ 6. I think I have gotten about as much as I deserve from life.

True___ False___ 7. I have not been bothered by many physical or emotional symptoms.

True___ False___ 8. I tend to trust most people without too much difficulty.

True___ False___ 9. Politicians are about as honest as the average person.

True___ False___ 10. I am probably no more sensitive than most people.

True___ False___ 11. It seldom occurs to me people might be laughing at me.

True___ False___ 12. Most people won't let you down in a pinch.

Assuming that you answered the questions the way you genuinely feel:

Count the number of Trues checked.

1. If you checked all twelve Trues, you have a very remarkable sense of self-acceptance.
2. Ten indicates a *high* degree of self-acceptance.
3. Eight is indicative of a *very good* degree of self-acceptance.
4. Six is *average*.
5. Anything below six suggests a *rather weak* self-image.